Cabin Style

Decorating with Rustic, Adirondack, and Western Collectibles

Schiffer Publishing Ltd

4880 Lower Valley Road, Atglen, PA 19310 USA

Dian Zillner and
Suzanne Silverthorn

Library of Congress Cataloging-in-Publication Data

Zillner, Dian.
  Cabin style : decorating with rustic, Adirondack, and western collectibles / by Dian Zillner and Suzanne Silverthorn.
      p. cm.
  ISBN 0-7643-2019-X (pbk.)
1. Decoration and ornament, Rustic—United States. 2. Collectibles in interior decoration—United States. I. Title.
NK1986.R8Z55 2004
747'.9—dc22
                                        2004001277

Copyright © 2004 by Dian Zillner and Suzanne Silverthorn

Designed by Ellen "Sue" Taltoan
Type set in Americana XBd BT/Humanst521 BT
ISBN: 0-7643-2019-X

Printed in China
1 2 3 4

Front cover (clockwise from top right): Collection of vintage radios. Thomas Molesworth chair, *courtesy of Fighting Bear Antiques*. Snowshoes in pack basket and boat seat, *courtesy of Avalanche Ranch*. Western lamp, *courtesy of Jim Shivers*. Back cover: Postcard of Old Faithful Inn, Yellowstone National Park. Spine photo: Fishing creels *courtesy of Bob Scott*. Contents Page: Chair made by Old Hickory Chair Co., *courtesy of Bob Scott*. Title page: Vintage hickory firewood holder, *courtesy of Avalanche Ranch*.

All of the items in this book are from private collections and museums. Grateful acknowledgment is made to the original producers of the materials photographed. The copyright has been identified for each item whenever possible. If any omission or incorrect information is found, please notify the author or publisher and it will be amended in any future edition of the book. The prices listed in these captions are intended only as a guide, and should not be used to set prices for any of the cabin collectibles pictured. Prices vary from one section of the country to another and also from dealer to dealer. The prices listed here are the best estimates the authors can give at the time of publication but prices in the field can change quickly. This is especially true with the added sales from the Internet. Neither the author nor the publisher assumes responsibility for any losses that might be incurred as a result of consulting this price guide.

Published by Schiffer Publishing Ltd.
4880 Lower Valley Road
Atglen, PA 19310
Phone: (610) 593-1777; Fax: (610) 593-2002
E-mail: Info@schifferbooks.com

For the largest selection of fine reference books on this and related subjects, please visit our web site at **www.schifferbooks.com**
We are always looking for people to write books on new and related subjects. If you have an idea for a book please contact us at the above address.

This book may be purchased from the publisher.
Include $3.95 for shipping.
Please try your bookstore first.
You may write for a free catalog.

In Europe, Schiffer books are distributed by
Bushwood Books
6 Marksbury Ave.
Kew Gardens
Surrey TW9 4JF England
Phone: 44 (0) 20 8392-8585; Fax: 44 (0) 20 8392-9876
E-mail: info@bushwoodbooks.co.uk
Free postage in the U.K., Europe; air mail at cost.

Dedication

A rustic cabin high in the Rocky Mountains provided the perfect setting for our family vacations as we headed West to escape the summer heat. The original homestead structure, even without electricity or indoor plumbing, allowed us to use our ingenuity to provide all the comforts of home. This book is dedicated to those happy memories.

Contents

Introduction

The authors' first Colorado log cabin purchased in 1965. The drawing was created by friend Marianne Wachter in 1966 during a family visit from Missouri.

We had our first experience with cabin living in the mid-1960s when the family purchased an old log cabin in Colorado for vacation use. The structure had been used by a woman suffering from tuberculosis with the hope that the Colorado climate would assist in improving her health. This didn't happen and after her death the cabin was traded to a new owner in exchange for some plumbing work done in Denver. The cabin remained in that family for many years until our purchase of the one-room home. It came with a few furnishings, including an old wood-burning cook stove that we used for warmth, heating water, and sometimes cooking (when our travel trailer's kitchen wasn't adequate). We had already furnished our regular Missouri home with antique walnut and oak furniture so the family was accustomed to attending auctions, casing thrift shops, and checking out antique stores to discover treasures. Thrift shop purchases for the cabin included a stripped oak kitchen cabinet, ready to finish priced at $18.00, and a set of five painted oak pressed back chairs for 35¢ each. Those were the days! That first rustic cabin provided the setting for several vacations filled with fun for both the family and visitors. It was the first of five cabins owned and enjoyed by the authors in the last forty years.

Those forty years don't begin to compare, however, to the many cabin owners who have vacationed in the same family summer home for generations. Colorado, Minnesota, and, of course, the Adirondacks are just three of the areas of the United States where summer homes have been part of the culture since the early part of the twentieth century.

The early Adirondacks homes have provided the most influence for the current interest in rustic décor. The Adirondacks are located in the northeast corner of New York state within a state park consisting of approximately six million acres. The park includes many small towns, including Lake Placid, a winter Olympics venue. Although the state of New York owns forty percent of the area, the rest of the acreage is privately held.

According to Craig Gilborn writing in his book *Adirondack Furniture and the Rustic Tradition,* the first Adirondacks developer was William West Durant, who began building Camp Pine Knot in the late 1870s. The camp included a lodge, dining facilities, and several cottages. All of the buildings were furnished with pieces made locally of bark, logs, and twigs. This was the beginning of the famous "camps" of the Adirondacks. Many wealthy people built "camps" during the late 1800s and early 1900s. Included were J.P. Morgan, Alfred G. Vanderbilt, and Marjorie Merriweather Post. These early estates (camps) consisted of many acres as well as large homes. The Adirondacks "look" included log construction, covered porches, stone fireplaces, and rustic furnishings made locally of twigs, logs, roots, and bark. In addition, the "camps" also imported Old Hickory furniture from Indiana. These pieces were used as both inside and outside furnishings in many homes. The inside décor of the "camps" included animal trophies that featured heads and hides of deer, elk, bear, and other wildlife.

By the depression years of the 1930s, the large "camps" were no longer as popular as they had been in earlier years. Because the places required so much upkeep, the camps were not as desirable. Some caught fire, acreage was sold from others, a few were allowed to deteriorate, and many were sold. It wasn't until the 1960s that interest was revived in the large camps that were left. Non-profit groups began to try to save some examples of the early camps and work was begun to place outstanding examples of the Adirondack Camps on the National Trust for Historic Places.

Although interest was being awakened in the East for the preservation of these homes, the Adirondack style was relatively unknown in the rest of the country, except for the few National Park lodges that still retained their architecture and some of the original interior décor and furnishings.

In the 1990s, perhaps because of the new interest in building log homes, the Adirondack "look" became popular with a more widespread audience. With this interest, old pieces of rustic furniture were retrieved from sheds and barns to begin new lives as important parts of a cabin's décor. Especially popular were pieces of Indiana hickory furniture dating from the earlier years. Wood-burning cooking and heating stoves were also refurbished to add to the nostalgic look in today's cabins. Animal trophies, camp blankets, pack baskets, creels, old sports equipment, Indian related items, and old souvenirs are just some of the items that have become popular for use in decorating a cabin to emphasize the rustic look.

In tandem with the revival of the rustic Adirondack style, the Western look has also been gaining popularity as a favored interior design for cabins. The most famous western designer was Thomas Molesworth, who founded the Shoshone Furniture Co. in Cody, Wyoming in 1931. *(See The Western Look chapter.)* Because most collectors can't afford furniture made by Molesworth, new interest has focused on the mass produced furniture of the 1950s that featured a Western look. In addition, the metal Monterrey Western Ware dishes, pot metal horses, vintage western clothing, and children's western themed toys have all gained in popularity during the last decade. Saddles, bridles, spurs, stirrups, and chaps are in great demand today as well, because of their authenticity.

Whether you are adding a rustic or western accent to a cabin's current décor or choosing to redecorate an entire home, we hope this book serves as a useful resource in creating a look that's right you. Over 500 photographs of various cabin collectibles are presented within the book's fifteen chapters, all illustrating items that can add personality and style to your decorating project. The chapters feature dishes, pottery, glassware, camp blankets, souvenirs, and furniture pieces that can provide interesting accents for any vacation or weekend getaway. Vintage sports, fishing, hunting, camping, and picnicking collectibles are pictured as well, and there is a special chapter on the Western look. Suggestions are also given on how to put the items to practical use, as well as ideas for displaying family items and relics. Original advertisements found in vintage catalogs and magazines from the early 1900s to the 1960s are used to trace the origins of many of these products. A bibliography, price guide, and source list also are included as helpful resources.

Many people have helped make this book possible. The authors express their appreciation to the individuals who answered questions, shared collectibles, and took photographs to assist with this book. A special thanks goes to Avalanche Ranch in Redstone, Colorado, and Little Bear's Antique Mall in Glenwood Springs, Colorado, who allowed us to photograph appropriate items from their shops. Bob Scott, Jim Shivers and the Grand Lake Lodge also gave the authors permission to photograph several of their collectibles. Others who helped with the book include: Daniel J. Bowater; Sharon Boucher; Bill Brewer; Betty Corbin; Fighting Bear Antiques, Jackson Hole, Wyoming (Terry and Sandy Winchell); Ardith and Don Finnicum; Chuck and Ann Fuller; Carolyn Geier and the Morgan County Public Library, Martinsville, Indiana; Harvey Gilmore; Grand Elk Marina and Beach Club, Granby, Colorado; Grand Lake Area Historical Society, Grand Lake, Colorado; Marjorie Huston Hermann; Caleb Hurtt; Sue James; Stewart Kelly; Glenn and Douglas Land; Loveland Public Library, Loveland, Colorado; Martinsville Indiana Chamber of Commerce (Bill Cunningham); Francy Mascarenas (Eagle Eye Photo, Eagle, Colorado); Marge Meisinger; Old Hickory Furniture Co., Shelbyville, Indiana (Bob Morrison); Jeff Oliver; Ruby I. Pettinger; Marilyn and Larry Pittman; Don Roslund; Wyatt Sabadosh; Deborah Taylor; Charles and Margaret Thornburg; Dick and Joyce Wolf; and Larry Zillner and family.

Thanks also to the members of our family for their patience and support with the preparation of this book. Mark Silverthorn helped with lighting and heavy moving; Jeff Zillner gave advice, answered questions, and assisted with editing; while Prather Silverthorn was again called into service to hold the lights.

Acknowledgment and extra recognition is also extended to Schiffer Publishing Ltd. and its excellent staff, particularly to Ellen "Sue" Taltoan, designer, and Ginny Parfitt, editor, who helped with this publication. Without their support and extra effort, this book would not have been possible.

Pinecone Decorated Pottery, Dinner, and Glassware

Nothing else conveys the splendor of cabin living more than the image of a pinecone. Its simplistic beauty and symbolism combine to make it a striking and timeless theme. The most frequent representation can be found in pottery, dinnerware, and glassware products that have been embellished with pinecone designs. The Roseville, McCoy, and Weller companies all used pinecone patterns during the first half of the twentieth century. While this pottery sold well, it was not until the 1950s and 1960s that many other firms began marketing pottery and dinnerware with similar pinecone features. Mail order catalogs featured some of these designs, which originated in both the United States and in Japan. Most of the new sets of dishes were quite inexpensive and some could be purchased at "dime" stores for as little as $2.50 for a five-piece place setting. Even the new plastic "Melmac" dishes were manufactured bearing pinecone images. A new pottery firm, "Rocky Mountain Pottery Co.," was also adding to the availability of pinecone designed items during this era. The company produced dinnerware as well as a large variety of other pottery pieces.

Fortunately for cabin owners, many sets or individual pieces of these dishes are relatively easy to find at reasonable prices. Acquiring these collectibles to use in a cabin as tableware or as accessories can make an interesting hobby.

The Syracuse China Co. produced its pinecone china primarily for commercial use in restaurants or hotels so it is heavier than regular dinnerware. It would be more time consuming to acquire a set of this china but pieces might be combined with other restaurant designs (some are marked with the actual place of business) to make an interesting table setting.

Although the Roseville, Weller, and Peters & Reed pinecone pottery is higher priced, examples from other firms from the 1950s and 1960s are relatively inexpensive and do not have the more formal look of the Roseville and Weller pieces.

Vintage table linens can also be acquired to accompany the sets of china from earlier years. Many designs were produced which pictured pinecones in various colors. Hand embroidered tablecloths in a variety of sizes, including those to be used on card tables, were also popular through the years. These may be harder to find in good condition. Fortunately, new tablecloths and place mats featuring pinecone motifs are readily available and can be used with the vintage dishes.

Glassware featuring pinecone designs has also been manufactured. Libbey and Douglas as well as other firms made a variety of sizes, styles, and colors of glasses to accompany the popular pinecone dishes.

Antique shops, flea markets, garage sales, and Internet auctions all offer great places to begin a hunt for these types of collectibles.

The following companies created pinecone decorated products during several decades of the twentieth century. Many of these firms are no longer in business.

Peters & Reed and McCoy pinecone decorated pottery pieces are pictured on an old wicker table with an oak top. The aqua and brown piece was made by McCoy while the other pottery was made by Peters & Reed.

Cannonsburg China Company
(Cannonsburg Pottery)

Cannonsburg China Company was located in Cannonsburg, Pennsylvania, from 1901 to 1978. In 1909, the company was purchased by a new corporation and the name was changed to Cannonsburg Pottery Company, according to Lois Lehner writing in *Lehner's Encyclopedia of U.S. Marks on Pottery, Porcelain and Clay*. John George (brother of W.S. George) was elected president of the new firm. Control of the company remained in the George family until 1976 when it was sold to Angelo Falconi. A fire in 1975 disabled the plant and a bankruptcy sale was held in 1978.

The firm produced various patterns of dinnerware throughout most of its existence. Cabin owner collectors are especially interested in the pinecone-designed set of semi-porcelain dinnerware, circa late 1950s to early 1960s. Another company design, which features pink clover, is sometimes referred to as a pinecone pattern, but many pieces are marked "Clover."

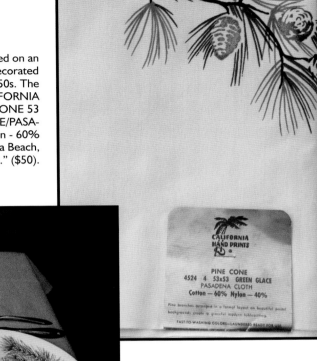

The dishes are displayed on an unused tablecloth also decorated with pinecones, circa 1950s. The label reads "CALIFORNIA HAND PRINTS/PINE CONE 53 X 53/GREEN GLACE/PASADENA CLOTH/Cotton - 60% Nylon - 40%/Hermosa Beach, California." ($50).

Cannonsburg Pottery dinnerware decorated with a very large pinecone design. The set includes four plates, four cups and saucers, four salad plates, four bowls, a platter, teapot, and cream and sugar. The plates are marked on the back "SIMPLICITY/ THE HALLMARK/CANNONSBURG/ OF QUALITY." A picture of a cannon is also part of the marking. (Set $60+).

French Saxon China Company

The French Saxon China Company was located in Sebring, Ohio. *Lehner's Encyclopedia of U.S. Marks on Pottery, Porcelain and Clay* attributes the early roots of the French Saxon China Company to the French China Company, which was founded circa 1900. According to author Lois Lehner, three china companies were consolidated in 1916. They included the French China Company, the Strong Manufacturing Company, and the Saxon China Company. The three firms kept their individual names as part of the Sebring Manufacturing Company. All three china lines ceased operations in the early 1930s. Lehner further states that the Saxon China Company was opened as the French Saxon China Company in 1934. The firm continued to produce semi-porcelain dinnerware until 1964, when it was purchased by the Royal China Company. The new owner may have retained the French Saxon China Company name on some items for a few more years.

The company produced an inexpensive set of pinecone decorated dishes in the late 1950s. This dinnerware was carried by the Woolworth "dime" stores. The dishes fit in nicely with the now popular rustic cabin look.

French Saxon "Pine Cone" dishes circa late 1950s. The dishes were carried by Woolworth "dime" stores. An original box contained the following information: "Shop your Woolworth Store First/16 Piece Starter Set/PINE CONE/4 dinner plates/4 desserts/4 cups/4 saucers/$3.98." Pictured is a place setting of these dishes which included a plate, cup and saucer, and dessert bowl. The plate is marked "French Saxon China" inside a shield with armor and swords through it. "U.S.A. 5/Pine Cone/2837-S54." Extra pieces could be purchased to complete the sets of dishes. (Setting, $25+).

A tidbit tray was also produced to accompany the set of pinecone French Saxon dishes. ($45).

W.S. George Pottery Co.

The W.S. George Pottery Co. was in business for over fifty years at several different locations, including East Palestine, Ohio; Cannonsburg, Pennsylvania; and Kittanning, Pennsylvania. According to author Loris Lehner, the founder of the pottery firm, William Shaw George, died in 1925, but the pottery enterprise continued with family members in charge through most of the 1950s. The last plant to close was the one in Cannonsburg, Pennsylvania. In the early years, the firm produced restaurant dishes as well as semi-porcelain dinnerware. The Montgomery Ward Fall and Winter catalog for 1955-56 advertised a set of pinecone decorated dishes called "Pinehurst" made by the W.S. George Pottery Co.

W.S. George Pinehurst dinnerware circa mid 1950s. The pinecone decorated dishes included the then popular "wing" look on the sides of each piece when possible. Included are a plate, cup and saucer, salad plate, sauce bowl, and soup bowl. The plate is marked "W.S. GEORGE/ HALF CENTURY FINE DINNERWARE/1904-1954." ($35-$40 place setting).

PINEHURST

Advertisement for Pinehurst semi-porcelain dinnerware pictured in the Montgomery Ward Fall and Winter catalog for 1955-1956. The pieces were made by the W.S. George Pottery Company. A 16-piece set was priced at $5.75 while a 53-piece set cost $19.95. Open stock serving pieces included the following: soup bowls, sauce dishes, covered sugar, creamer, covered vegetable dish, gravy boat and stand, medium and large platters, open vegetable dish, tea or coffee server, salt and pepper shakers, and salad plates.

Hall China Company

The Hall China Company was located in East Liverpool, Ohio. Robert Hall and his son Robert T. Hall founded the business in 1903. After Robert Hall's death, his son took over the firm.

The company prospered over the years and is still in business. The firm has become well known for its line of teapots, pitchers, kitchenware, dinnerware, and the Autumn Leaf line produced as premiums for the Jewel Tea Company.

Less well known are the Hall China "Hallcraft" pieces from the 1950s. Eva Zeisel designed the shapes of the lines, while Charles Seliger created some of the patterns. These designs included Fantasy, Harlequin, Arizona, Mulberry, Peach Blossom, Fern, and Bouquet.

The pinecone decorated dinnerware is of special interest to cabin owners. Recently, after Zeisel unearthed the lost Hallcraft molds, she announced that she hoped to be able to find a company interested in producing a new line of the dishes.

Pinecone "Hallcraft" bowls are from the dinnerware designed by Eva Zeisel in the 1950s. The bowls are marked "HALLCRAFT/By Eva Zeisel/ MADE In U.S.A. by HALL CHINA CO." Several different patterns were produced including this pinecone design. ($25-$30 each).

Harker Pottery platter circa late 1950s to early 1960s. This unusual pinecone design features black pinecones and stems instead of the more usual brown. The platter is marked "Harkerware since 1840" in a square. Under the square is "East Liverpool, Ohio." Above the square is "Harker Pottery." ($30-$35).

Heavy weight cup, saucer, and plate made for commercial use. The dishes feature a pinecone motif. The plate is marked "JACKSON CHINA/Falls Creek, PA." (The 3 pieces come from a setting for 5 totaling 15 pieces for $145). *Courtesy of Avalanche Ranch, Redstone, Colorado.*

Harker Pottery

Harker Pottery was located in East Liverpool, Ohio, and was in business from 1840 to 1972. It was established by Benjamin Harker, Sr. After a variety of name changes and family members in and out of the business, the firm was incorporated as the Harker Pottery Co. in 1890. According to Lois Lehner, Harker began making pottery and dinnerware that could be used in the oven as early as the late 1920s. The firm continued this practice until they ended business in 1972. The company also made collectible dinnerware patterns called Cameoware, White Rose, and Dainty Flower. In the late 1950s to early 1960s, Harker offered an unusual set of pinecone decorated dishes as part of its line. The pattern featured black pinecones and stems instead of the more usual brown.

In 1972 the company was sold to the Jeannette Glass Company.

Jackson China Co.

Jackson China Co. began business in Falls Creek, Pennsylvania in 1917 under the name Jackson Vitrified China Company. The firm was incorporated in 1920, according to Lois Lehner writing in Lehner's *Encyclopedia of U.S. Marks on Pottery, Porcelain and Clay*. In 1946, the plant's equipment was updated and a larger workforce was hired. When a new owner purchased the firm in 1976 the name was changed to Jackson China, Inc. By the 1980s, all of the china production was sold to institutions, including hotels, restaurants, etc. By this time, new owners had once again taken over the business.

Libbey Glass Company

The Libbey Glass Company is located in Toledo, Ohio. It was established by Edward Libbey in 1888. The firm produced cut glass in the early years. The Libbey Glass Company is still in business today.

More recent silver pinecone patterned glasses made by Libbey Glass in Toledo, Ohio. Each glass is marked with an "L." Some of the company boxes have been marked "Libbey, America's Oldest Glassmaker First in Ideas Since 1818." (See also page 24). ($20-$25 set).

Loveland Art Pottery

Loveland Art Pottery was located in Loveland, Colorado, and produced pottery from approximately 1948 until 1969. The firm was founded by Helmer Roslund, who had already worked in the pottery business for many years. As a young man, Roslund emigrated to the U.S. from Sweden. His pottery experience began at the Red Wing Potteries in Red Wing, Minnesota, where he worked for twenty-five years. He then moved to Camden, Arkansas, to continue pottery making for CAMARK. Four years later, in 1948, Roslund relocated to Loveland, Colorado, where he began his own business. The new firm was located at 350 South Lincoln Avenue. Tourists using Highway 287 during trips to Rocky Mountain National Park became good customers. The business eventually grew large enough that two salesmen were employed to sell the pottery along with other lines they were representing.

Roslund's son Don also worked for the firm for the first nine years. Loveland Pottery was very successful from the mid to late 1950s. The most popular pieces produced by the firm were those which featured hand painted pinecone designs beginning in the early 1950s. Most of these items were made on a white background with brown and green decorations. The pottery with a light brown background decorated with dark brown pinecones was also popular. In addition, the company made dinnerware in a white and green swirl pattern in a modern cosmos style. The firm always produced pieces for florists, which became a big part of the business. Most of these items were sold wholesale.

The pottery was closed circa 1969-1970 upon the death of the founder. Until then, it had always remained a small business with four or five people plus the salesmen working to make Loveland Art Pottery memorable. *Information courtesy of Don Roslund.*

Loveland Art Pottery hand painted ring box, circa 1950s. Marked on the bottom with a sticker reading "Loveland Art Pottery/ Loveland, Colo." ($15+).

Three pieces of Loveland Art Pottery showing some of the different colors used in producing pinecone decorated pieces, circa 1950s. The firm marked its pottery in several different ways. The cup has "LOVELAND/POTTERY" incised on its bottom. The aqua vase is marked with a sticker, which reads "LOVELAND/ART POTTERY/Loveland, Colo." The brown vase is incised "LOVELAND POTTERY." (Prices range from $10-$15 for the cup, to $15-$18 for the vases).

Loveland Art Pottery wall pocket in an unusual design, circa 1950s. The pocket appears to be decorated with ridges instead of finished with a flat surface. The well-known pinecone design is also present. It is incised on the back "LOVELAND/ART POTTERY/122." ($35+).

Loveland Art Pottery tidbit dish decorated with pinecones and a deer. Unlike Rocky Mountain Pottery's similar pieces, which include removable deer, this one is permanently attached to the dish. All of the Loveland pottery's pinecone pieces were hand painted. This piece is unmarked. ($35-$45).

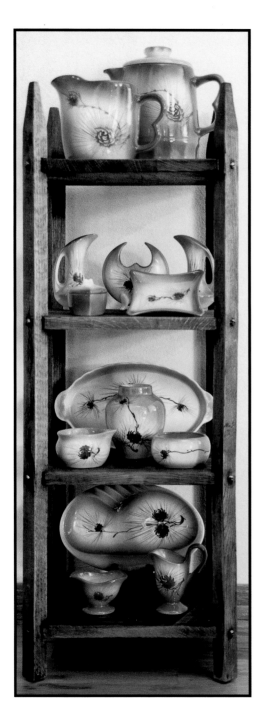

Various pieces of Loveland Art Pottery, decorated in the pinecone design, fill a small oak shelf unit. Included are pitchers, cream and sugar sets, heart shaped ring box, vases, and small trays. The matching pieces are marked with either the company stickers or are incised "Loveland Art Pottery" on the undersides.

Two Loveland pitchers show the similarity and the differences in their designs. Although both pitchers have the same type handles, the spouts are entirely different. The painted designs on both pitchers are very similar while the bottoms of the pitchers differ. The smaller pitcher is marked "173." The coffee pot is incised "Loveland Art Pottery/146." ($35-$45 each).

Marshall Burns Inc. (Mar-Crest)

Marshall Burns Inc. was located in Chicago, Illinois, according to Lois Lehner from the book *Lehner's Encyclopedia of U.S. Marks on Pottery, Porcelain and Clay*. The firm was a sales agency, which contracted with various companies to have products manufactured for their distribution. During the 1950s and early 1960s, the firm handled both ceramic dinnerware and stoneware, including Mar-Crest pinecone decorated ceramic dinnerware.

Original Mar-Crest box which contained a five-piece place setting of hand painted oven proof dinnerware. The other information on the box states that the set is "From the potteries of Marshall-Burns, Inc. Chicago, 54 Illinois." The original price for the 5-piece set was $2.50. The box is also marked with the pattern name "Pine."

Mar-Crest circa late 1950s five-piece place setting contained in the original box. Included are a dinner plate, salad plate, dessert dish, cup and saucer. The bottom of the plate is marked "Oven Proof Dinnerware/Hand painted/Under glaze/ Made in U.S.A." The cup is marked only "MADE IN USA." ($15-$18 per box).

Nelson McCoy Pottery

Nelson McCoy Pottery was located in Roseville, Ohio. According to *Warman's Antiques and Price Guide: 37th Edition*, it was founded by Nelson McCoy in 1910 as the Nelson McCoy Sanitary Stoneware Company (later becoming known as the Nelson McCoy Pottery Company). Authors Sharon and Bob Huxford state that McCoy remained the head of the firm until he died in 1945, then son Nelson McCoy, Jr., took over as president and retained that job for many years. The firm was sold in the 1960s but apparently continued in business until 1985.

The McCoy products have remained popular with collectors. Cookie jars, tea sets, and jardinières are among the favorites.

The "McCoy" impressed mark was used beginning in the 1940s; later, "U.S.A." was added below the mark. The same mark when embossed indicates the piece was made from the mid 1940s to the 1960s.

Two lines of the McCoy Pottery are of special interest to cabin decorators: the "Rustic" pieces from the mid 1940s and the pinecone tea set, circa 1946. Sharon and Bob Huxford, authors of *The Collectors Encyclopedia of McCoy Pottery*, write that McCoy was "considered to be the nation's leading manufacturer of artwear" during the firm's later years.

McCoy "Rustic" 7" tall planter featuring embossed pinecones, needles, and stems finished in aqua and brown. "McCoy" is embossed on the bottom. Circa mid 1940s. ($35-$40).

McCoy Pinecone pattern tea set with a covered teapot, creamer, and open sugar bowl, circa 1946. Marked with an embossed "McCoy" on the bottom of each piece. ($90-$100 set).

Paden City Pottery

Paden City Pottery offices were in Paden City, West Virginia. The company was in business from 1914 until 1963, manufacturing semi-porcelain dinnerware. The firm used decals on its china instead of painting the design by hand. Two designs of pinecone decorated dishes were offered by the firm circa late 1950s to early 1960s. One featured unusual aqua pinecones while the other dinner set motif consisted of the more usual brown pinecones.

Paden City Pottery platter circa late 1950s or early 1960s featuring a decal design of aqua pinecones. Marked on back: "The Paden City Pottery Co./Made in U.S.A/Oven Proof/H-56." ($15-$20).

Paden City saucer and salt and pepper shakers featuring a different pinecone design, circa late 1950s. The saucer is marked: "Eden Roc China Co." According to Lois Lehner from the book *Lehner's Encyclopedia of U.S. Marks on Pottery, Porcelain and Clay*, this was a trade name used by Paden City Pottery in the 1950s. (Salt and pepper shakers $10-$12, saucer $2-$3).

Peters & Reed

Peters & Reed was located in Zanesville, Ohio, and was incorporated circa 1901 by John D. Peters and Adam Reed. At first, the small company produced flower pots, but circa 1910 it entered the art pottery field. Designer Frank Ferrell developed the "Moss Aztec" line in 1912, which became very successful. Many of these pieces were produced featuring pinecone designs. In 1921, according to *Warman's Antiques and Collectibles Price Guide: 37th Edition*, the company became Zane Pottery and continued in business until 1941. None of the early pieces produced by Peters & Reed appear to be marked.

Peters & Reed Moss Aztec vessel with raised pinecones and needles decoration. 4.25" high x 7.5" in diameter. Unmarked. ($50+).

Peters & Reed Moss Aztec jardinière, 9" high x 11" in diameter, decorated with relief molded pinecone decorations on brown ground with green accents. Signed by designer Frank Ferrell, otherwise unmarked. ($200+).

Rocky Mountain Pottery Company

The Rocky Mountain Pottery Company was located in Loveland, Colorado, after an earlier beginning in Denver. The company was founded by Leland (Lee) Huston in 1953 and was moved to Loveland in 1957. The firm's first pottery pieces were produced to resemble wood grain and included a pine scent. Anticipating the pottery's appeal to tourists, the firm's new factory was strategically located in Loveland along Highway 34 on the way to Rocky Mountain National Park. Since the pottery was produced on site, tourists were encouraged to take tours to see how the pieces were made. The most popular product was the pine-scented ashtray, which sold for 98¢. The Rocky Mountain scented wood grained pieces could be found in gift shops servicing National Parks in the western part of the country for many years. Surprisingly, the Wall Drug Store in South Dakota was the best wholesale customer for the company. For a short time after opening the factory in Loveland, a paper label was used on the pottery reading, "Designed and Manufactured by the Lee Craft Pottery Co., Loveland, Colorado."

In the late 1950s (circa 1956-1957) the pottery with hand painted pinecone designs was developed. The first pieces featured a white background with an added pinecone design. The insides of these early pieces were green. The familiar specks were added to the outsides of the pinecone pottery circa 1961-1962. The pinecone line was then expanded to include three colors, off white,

brown, and aqua. Besides a variety of vases, planters, ashtrays, candlesticks, mugs, pitchers, and snack sets, the firm also produced birds and deer figures. In addition to these items, dinnerware was made in the three colors. Pieces included plates, cups, saucers, salad plates, soup bowls, glasses, several sizes of vegetable bowls (including one divided to hold two different vegetables), several sizes and designs of platters, creamer and sugar bowl, salt and pepper shakers, covered butter dish, gravy boat, relish dish, coffeepot, teapot with stand, and a fondue pot with stand. The forty-five piece dinnerware set with settings for eight remained in the line for ten years or more.

Personalized mugs in the pinecone designs were big sellers. The gift shop inventory included nearly a thousand different mugs and employees added other names when requests were made. These mugs served as popular and inexpensive souvenirs to take home from a Colorado vacation.

Many other pottery designs were produced by the Rocky Mountain Pottery Company, but the most popular lines throughout the Huston years remained the pine-scented wood grained design and the various colors of the hand painted pinecone line.

The late 1960s and 1970s were the most successful years for the Huston owned Rocky Mountain Pottery Co. During the summers in many of those years, the Loveland factory employed thirty-five to forty people and tours for tourists were conducted from 7:00 a.m. until 7:00 p.m. each day. Two other outlets also sold the pottery each summer. One was located in Estes Park, Colorado, and the other was in Colorado Springs. Rocky Mountain Pottery acquired a plant in Eastland, Texas, circa 1961-62, and it made other lines of pottery that were also sold at the Colorado outlets.

The Rocky Mountain Pottery factory was sold to Bill and Louise Green circa 1981 upon the Huston's retirement to California. The Greens eventually made some changes to the business to incorporate their interest in weaving. The Greens sold the Rocky Mountain Pottery factory in 1986 to Lee and Linda Shultz and the original business came to an end.

Information courtesy of Marjorie Hermann (formerly Marjorie Huston, wife of founder), Charles Thornburg (Rocky Mountain Pottery plant manager for many years), his wife Margaret, and Stewart Kelly (designer of many pottery pieces at the factory).

Shelf full of wood grained, pine scented pottery made by the Rocky Mountain Pottery Company in Loveland, Colorado. Besides vases, planters, and other usual items, the firm also produced a variety of figures including deer, ducks, owls, turkeys, cats, a cowboy boot, and many other items.

Two Rocky Mountain Pottery ash trays, including the 98¢ one on the right that was the best selling item the firm sold. It carries an early paper label which reads "Designed and Manufactured by the Lee Craft Pottery Co. Loveland Colorado." Also marked in black on the bottom "Made in the Rockies." ($5-$7 each).

The larger pine scented ash tray carries the incised "ROMCO" mark used on much of the pottery during owner Lee Houston's years.

Rocky Mountain Pottery wood grained, pine scented vases showing the different looks of the wood grained design. Some of the items are not marked while others are stamped "Made in the Rockies" or incised with the ROMCO trademark. The later sticker was black with gold trim and read "Handcrafted /in/Colorado/by Rocky Mountain Pottery." (Prices range from $6-$15 each depending on size).

Two of the first Rocky Mountain Pottery pieces produced with hand painted pinecone designs. The planters are finished in white with green insides and decorated with hand painted pinecone designs. The earlier items did not include the overlay of specks of color, which were added later. The green finish on the inside was also eliminated when different colors joined the line. Neither piece is marked. ($8-$10 each).

Rocky Mountain Pottery sets of glasses in the three pinecone pottery colors made by the firm. The hand painted sets could be purchased in either six glass or eight glass combinations along with the pottery carrier. The bottom of the holders are marked with an artist's palette with "ROMCO" incised inside. (Holders with six glasses, $50-$60; with eight glasses $65-$75).

The Rocky Mountain Pottery teapot and holder (perhaps a candle was to be placed under the holder) along with the coffeepot are some of the hardest pinecone items to find. These also were made in the three different colors. The coffeepot is marked with the artist palette marking and the teapot is unmarked. ($50-$65 each).

Oak shelf filled with Rocky Mountain aqua pottery featuring the pinecone design. Several pieces from the dinnerware set are pictured including a plate, bowl, cream and sugar, salt and pepper shakers, and covered butter dish. Some of the items are not marked while others are stamped "Made in the Rockies" or incised with the ROMCO trademark. (Prices range from $15-$30 except for the coffee and teapots).

Rocky Mountain Pottery table setting of off-white dinnerware featuring hand painted pinecone designs. The 45-piece dinnerware sets for eight were carried by the firm for ten years or more in off-white, aqua, and brown, all featuring the hand painted pinecone designs. The silverware is new. (The pieces pictured range in price from $8-$18 each.)

The shelves of this old oak school cabinet contain Rocky Mountain Pottery in the brown pinecone design. Included are: vases, salt and pepper shakers, pitchers, cream and sugar, candle sticks, planters, tea pot, glasses, and bowls. The brown sugar bowl includes a sticker which reads "This is an Original/By the Artists of/Rocky Mountain/Pottery Co./Colo. Springs/Estes Park/Loveland, Colorado." ($15-$40 each).

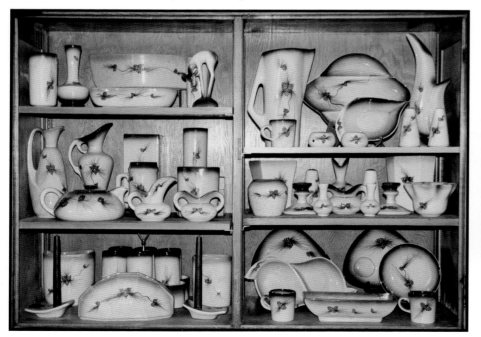

Antique oak file drawers and an old post office piece have been used as backdrops in the display of a collection of off-white Rocky Mountain Pottery. The brown trim on the pottery blends nicely with the oak wood.

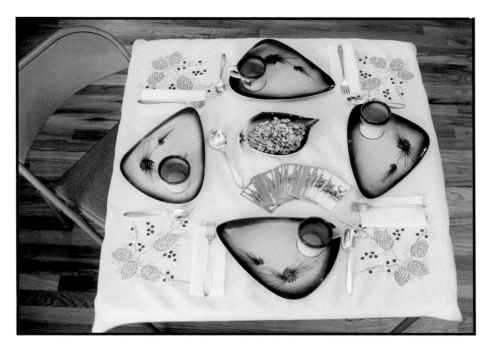

A vintage hand embroidered tablecloth, made to fit a card table, provides the proper background for a Rocky Mountain snack set in the brown pinecone pattern. These types of snack sets were popular during the 1950s into the 1970s to use for refreshments served at card parties. (Snack sets for four, $50).

Roseville Pottery Company

The Roseville Pottery Company was first located in Roseville, Ohio, when it was incorporated in 1892. The firm moved to Zanesville, Ohio, in 1898. George F. Young became head of the company and the Young family controlled the firm until the 1950s. According to *Warman's Antiques and Collectibles Price Guide: 37th Edition*, Frank Ferrell, who also designed pottery for Peters & Reed, developed many lines of pottery for Roseville beginning in 1918. He worked at the plant until it ceased operation in 1954.

The Roseville firm continued to prosper even during the depression years of the 1930s, when the Pinecone line was developed, circa 1935. According to Betty Ward and Nancy Schiffer in their book *Weller, Roseville and Related Zanesville Art Pottery and Tiles*, the line was based on an earlier design by Ferrell. There were seventy-five pieces in the Pinecone line and it became the most popular line the Roseville firm ever produced. The pinecone pieces were sold by the company for fifteen years. According to Schiffer and Ward, the line was revived in 1953.

In the 1930s, the Roseville Pottery was marked "Roseville" impressed on the bottom along with the pattern number. After 1939, "Roseville/U.S.A." along with the pattern number and size was embossed on the bottom to mark the pieces.

After World War II, business declined and the firm ceased operation in 1954.

Roseville Pottery 5" tall vase in the Pinecone pattern circa 1930s. The green vase is set off center and is decorated with a pinecone and pine needle handle. Impressed on the bottom is "Roseville/124." Roseville pottery pinecone bowl embossed on the bottom "Roseville/U.S.A./425-6," circa 1940s. Embossed pines decorate both the front and back of the bowl. (Vase $150-$175; bowl $175-$200).

Stetson China Company

The Stetson China Company was located in Lincoln, Illinois, from the 1930s until 1966 when it stopped production. Through the years, the firm changed from a decorator and distributing company to a dinnerware manufacturer. According to Lois Lehner writing in *Lehner's Encyclopedia of U.S. Marks on Pottery, Porcelain and Clay*, the firm boasted in 1955 advertisements that it was the largest manufacturer of individual hand-painted ceramic dinnerware in the United States.

Like so many other dinnerware makers, the Stetson firm also produced pinecone decorated pieces in the mid to late 1950s. Both an aqua pattern and a brown and green pinecone design were used on their dishes.

Stetson China Company small platter, cream pitcher, and sugar bowl featuring brown and green pinecone designs. These pieces are from a set of dishes circa mid to late 1950s. Platter marked on the back "Oven Proof/Dinnerware/Hand Decorated/Underglaze/Made in U.S.A." A paint brush was also included in the marking. (Platter $15-$20, cream and sugar pair, $15-$20).

This small platter is exactly the same size and shape as the previous Stetson piece. The pinecones on this platter are aqua. It is marked "Hand Decorated/Made in America/Oven Proof/Detergent Proof – Underglazed." Thought to be circa early 1960s. ($10-$15).

Syracuse China Company

The Syracuse China Company was located in Syracuse, New York. It was first known as Empire Pottery beginning in 1855. By 1871, the firm was using the Onondaga Pottery Company name. In 1966, the official name of the firm became Syracuse China Company. Even though many pieces of its china carried a Syracuse China mark beginning in 1879, according to Lois Lehner of *Lehner's Encyclopedia of U.S. Marks on Pottery, Porcelain and Clay*, the name of the firm wasn't changed to match the mark until 1966.

The firm produced dinnerware as well as other products for nearly one hundred years but discontinued this practice in 1970. The company then concentrated on commercial tableware, which had been a successful business for many years. The china decorated with pinecone designs is especially appealing to cabin owners.

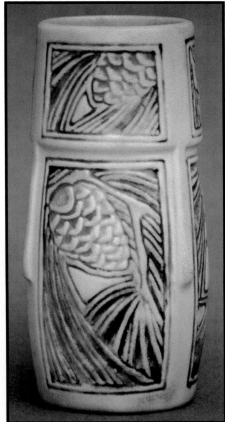

Weller vase in the Roma pattern, 7" tall, circa 1920s. The piece is decorated with panels of pinecones in brown and green. The vase is unmarked. ($100-$125).

Unmarked jardinière approximately 7" tall and 7.5" in diameter, attributed to Weller. It is decorated with raised pinecones and needles on a brown ground. ($150-$175).

Syracuse China plate marked "Syracuse China/3-A USA." It is heavy-duty restaurant ware which features an interesting pinecone decoration. The 3-A indicates when the piece was produced. In this case, it was probably made in January 1974. ($25-$30).

Syracuse China cup and saucer marked "Syracuse China/5-K." This is another pinecone pattern the firm made for commercial use. The 5-K mark indicates it was produced in November 1976. ($30-$35).

Weller Pottery

Weller Pottery was located in various places in Zanesville, Ohio, from approximately 1882 until 1948. The company was founded by Samuel A. Weller. The firm's art pottery lines were developed circa late 1800s through the World War I years. They included the Louwelsa and Sicard lines.

After the war, new lines, including Roma and Woodcraft, were developed. Some of the Roma pieces were decorated with raised pinecone designs. The company continued to grow until the depression years of the 1930s. The pottery business was revived during World War II but the company again faced hard times after the war and, according to *Warman's Antiques and Price Guide: 37th Edition,* the production of Weller Pottery ended in 1948.

Miscellaneous

In addition to all the well-known pottery companies, other pinecone decorated products were produced by lesser known firms. Included were vases, Melmac plastic dishes in a variety of pinecone designs, plus glasses, coffeepots, and carafes.

Four glasses and a carafe decorated with gold pinecones with aqua highlights, circa 1960s, from David Douglas. Marked "Douglas." ($15-$18 set).

Matching David Douglas coffeepot also finished in gold and aqua. ($12-$15).

A "Park Avenue" pinecone Melmac plate decorated with a pinecone design, circa early 1960s. The back of the plate is marked "Park Avenue/Melmac." ($3).

Set of six glasses made by the Libbey Glass Co. which feature a green and brown pinecone design. These types of glasses do not hold up well in a dishwasher as the designs eventually disappear. (See also page 11). (Glasses only, set of six, $20+).

Kitchen Collectibles

Old copper kitchen accessories can be given a new life when used in decorating a modern cabin. A single tea kettle or a collection can be displayed on an old gas or wood stove. Most of these kettles originally were plated with nickel or chrome. When the plating is removed, the copper is visible. These tea kettles sold for only $1.27 in the mid-1930s. Copper boilers can also add interest to a log cabin or home. A boiler can be placed next to a fireplace or wood stove to hold wood, filled with an assortment of pillows to add color, or used to hold a variety of vintage photo albums or scrapbooks. (Tea kettle, $30; boiler $50-$60).

Of all the rooms in a home, the kitchen offers one of the best places to display and integrate the use of cabin related collectibles. While pinecone decorated pottery and dinnerware is pictured in the *Glassware chapter,* canisters, enamelware, and other kitchen items in appropriate designs are shown in this chapter.

Besides accessories and useable smaller items, today's cabin kitchen can provide a place to display or use old kitchen appliances. With reproductions of these products now available, the demand for the old appliances may diminish, although some cabin owners will still prefer using authentic pieces. Many of the old stoves can be found in good working condition and there are some businesses that specialize in the repair and sale of these old appliances. Before deciding on the functional use of an old stove or ice box, owners should think about the amount of food preparation that will be done in the home. A cabin that is used only on weekends or brief vacations, for example, will not need as much food storage or as many modern conveniences as a kitchen in a home that is used as a full-time residence. There is one particular brand of vintage stove, however, that is in high demand, especially by gourmet cooks. It is the Imperial Chambers, a heavy gas stove, which was produced from the 1920s through the 1940s. Collectors prefer the large stoves with as many as six or eight burners. These stoves were usually sold for commercial use in churches or inns. The stoves were manufactured in Shelbyville, Indiana, after John Chambers founded the firm in 1912. Production continued until 1955.

For those who prefer new appliances, an older stove or ice box can still be added as a decorative accent. For example, an old oak refrigerator could be displayed in any room and used for storage or to house a television or CD player. Although many of the old wood-burning cook stoves were enormous, there are some models that are small enough to be added to a room's décor as a reminder of the way things used to be. These stoves can provide display space for copper tea kettles, old iron cookware, enamelware, or graniteware to add to the old fashioned look. Both granite and enamelware came in a variety of colors and these pieces can add interest when placed on a kitchen counter or in the space between the top of the cabinets and the ceiling. The stoves can also be placed on a covered porch to be used to hold pots of plants or flowers.

Some cabin owners may want to assemble a collection of old kitchen utensils to use as wall decorations. Ice tongs, soup ladles, large wooden spoons, iron skillets, potato mashers, water dippers, egg whips, rolling pins, and egg beaters can be combined to make an interesting wall arrangement. Old wash boards, sad irons, clothes wringers, and wood ironing boards could also be used for display in a laundry room in a large log home.

In addition to the old kitchen collectibles, newer kitchen accessories from the 1950s to the 1970s can be collected to add interest to a cabin kitchen. Many of these items were decorated with pinecones. Several different firms produced metal canister sets, bread boxes, and other items decorated with pinecone designs. Included were those by Ransburg and Deco Ware. A later pinecone decorated canister set (circa 1970s) was made of wood.

Older cabin related glassware can also be found, and both used and displayed in a cabin kitchen. Included are pieces decorated with ducks or geese. The patterns were produced in a variety of glass sizes, plus cocktail shakers, ice buckets, and pitchers. To provide a more wintry look for a ski lodge, vintage glasses picturing skiers or deer can be collected. If a cabin caters to a summer decor, pitchers and glasses featuring sailboats are particularly appropriate. Several sizes of blue depression glasses, an ice bucket, and a pitcher were produced by the Hazel Atlas Glass Co. Harder to find are sets of dinnerware which feature a sailboat motif. Like the blue sailboat glasses, these were also popular

in the 1930s. Several designs of refrigerator dishes and bowls also featured sailboat scenes during the 1930s. Most of these were produced by the McKee Co.

Old wildlife decorated plates and platters can also be used to decorate kitchen walls. The ones made by Buffalo Pottery are especially collectible. *(See Taxidermy and Wildlife Pictorials chapter.)*

Souvenir spoons can be displayed on a spoon rack in any room, but a kitchen or dining area is especially appropriate. The old sterling silver spoons can be found to complement many cabin themes. Especially popular are those images which feature sailboats, Indians, cowboys, wildflowers, a variety of wildlife, various states, National Parks, and resort towns. Any of these spoons could be used to enhance cabin décor. *(See Souvenirs chapter.)*

Be it modern or rustic, the basic cabin kitchen provides ample opportunities to showcase a variety of vintage collectibles.

This kitchen wall incorporates several types of kitchen collectibles into one arrangement. Included are pottery pieces made by the Rocky Mountain Pottery Co., old plates featuring scenes of deer and elk *(See Taxidermy and Wildlife Pictorials chapter)*, and souvenir spoons. Also displayed are vintage deer antlers, an elk picture in an oak frame, and a modern clock decorated with an elk in a mountain scene.

An oak ice box, circa 1910, which features a top opening for the ice and a front opening for food storage. Similar pieces could be used for storage or to provide space for a television on the bottom and a DVD player or VCR on top. This old refrigerator is lined with galvanized tin and is marked "Refrigerator/Cold-Dry Air/Chicago-New York." ($325-$350). *From the collection of the Larry Zillner family.*

A much larger wood burning cook stove was advertised in the Sears Fall and Winter 1935-1936 catalog. It came in two sizes priced at $59.50 and $67.50. These later stoves were finished in porcelain enamel with mostly cast iron construction and were "modern" in design.

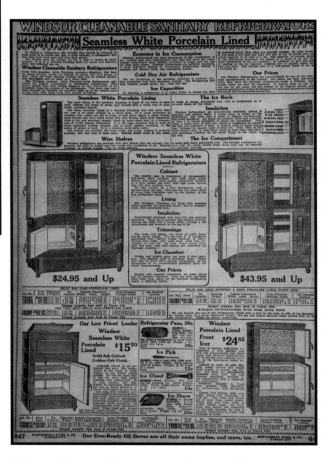

Wood burning cook stoves have been produced for over a hundred years and are still being made today. Although not too many households still choose to cook on these stoves, they can give an authentic old fashioned look to a modern kitchen. Most of the early stoves were quite large but smaller examples were also produced which may offer a more sensible range of possibilities for decorating a cabin kitchen. This one measures 52" high to top of back x 34" wide x 24" deep and features two burners, a griddle, an oven, and a wood receptacle. It includes a regulator on the oven door. The stove was manufactured by Eureka and it is made mostly of iron. A copper tea kettle and vintage bowl decorate the top of the stove. (Stove, $450).

By the 1920s cook stoves were being made to use gas as their fuel. The design for most of these stoves included four, tall narrow legs to offer support. The outside of the pictured stove was finished with porcelain enamel in green and ivory. It included an oven, broiler, utensil drawer, and four cook top burners. This advertisement appeared in the Sears Fall and Winter catalog for 1931-1932. The stove sold for $53.75.

Similar ice boxes to the one pictured on page 26 were advertised in the Montgomery Ward catalog circa 1916 for $15.50. Already, the boxes had been improved to include white porcelain linings. The "refrigerators" came in a variety of sizes and styles. The most expensive box was $43.95.

An assortment of copper boilers were advertised in the Sears 1935-36 Fall and Winter catalog. The most expensive was priced (with lid) for $2.98. The boilers were originally used to heat water, mostly for washing clothes.

The old oak ice boxes were no longer in style by the 1920s and new models were made of white metal with 1.5" of insulation separating the outside from the white enameled food space. By the 1930s electric refrigerators were in use which included a small freezer section to make ice cubes. This Cold Spot electric refrigerator was advertised in the Sears Fall and Winter catalog for 1935-1936. It sold for $137.95. During the depression years that was a lot of money, but Sears made it easier to purchase by letting the buyer pay $5 down and $8.50 each month, which brought the total cost to $151.75.

Vintage gas cooking stove and electric refrigerator currently used in a weekend cabin. The stove is circa late 1920s while the refrigerator is thought to be an early 1930s model. The oven door of the stove is marked "Universal." The stove is also imprinted "Cribben & Sexton Co. Chicago." It included four burners, oven, and a storage space. The vintage electric refrigerator was made by Frigidaire. It contains a small freezer compartment for ice cubes. (Stove, $375; refrigerator, $150).

Vintage graniteware also offers interesting pieces to accessorize a cabin kitchen. The granite came in several colors, but the most prevalent and easiest to find is gray. Blue still remains the most popular choice for collectors. Coffee pots, tea kettles, covered sauce pans, pie plates, cups, pails, wash basins, plates, and dishpans are just some of the items produced in granite. Pictured is a vintage coffee pot of gray graniteware with a black lid and wire and wood handle. ($50-$60).

Tea kettle, coffee pot, and cup, cream and green enamelware similar to that pictured in the Sears 1931-1932 Fall and Winter catalog. This particular color combination is especially collectible and pieces could be used individually or as part of a collection to add vintage touches to a cabin kitchen. (Tea kettle, with some wear, $25-$35; near mint coffee pot, $65+, cup, $15).

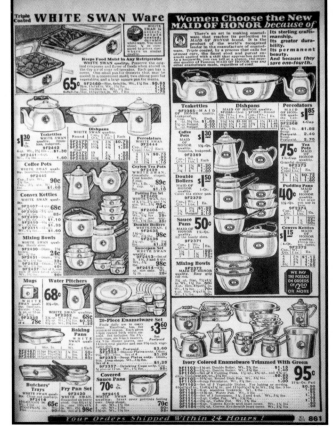

The Sears Fall and Winter catalog for 1931-1932 offered a whole page of enamelware for sale. Two company names were listed as providing the products: White Swan Ware and Maid of Honor. Most enamelware was white with an added trim of black, blue, or red. On the lower right are additional pieces that were ivory colored with a green trim. Included were a tea kettle, two types of coffee pots, covered pans, bucket, double boiler, sauce pan, and a dish pan. *(See also Vintage Camping and Picnicking Equipment chapter.)*

White enamelware trimmed in red or black are the easiest pieces to find. Shown are a coffee pot, cup, handled pan, wash bowl, and flat pan. (Coffee pot, $15-$20; cup, $5-$8; other items, $5-$10 each).

Another pinecone decorated metal canister set, circa 1960s. This later unmarked example features knobs and a non-traditional pinecone design. It is not known if this company made any other matching items. ($25 set).

Pinecone decorated metal bread box, hot pads, and two canisters from a four-piece set, circa 1950s. The bread box is marked "Deco Ware." A cake cover, match holder, and other additional matching items may have been produced. A collection of the various pieces of this set would add color and nostalgia to a cabin kitchen. (Hot pads, $5-$8 each; four-piece canister set, $35-$45; bread box, $35-$45).

The most expensive metal pinecone decorated kitchen canisters and bread boxes are those produced by RANSBURG in Indianapolis, Indiana, circa late 1950s to early 1960s. The pale yellow bread box and canisters are marked "Ransburg/Genuine/Hand Painted/Indianapolis/Made in U.S.A." They are especially collectible because they were hand painted. (Set with bread box wear, $100-$115).

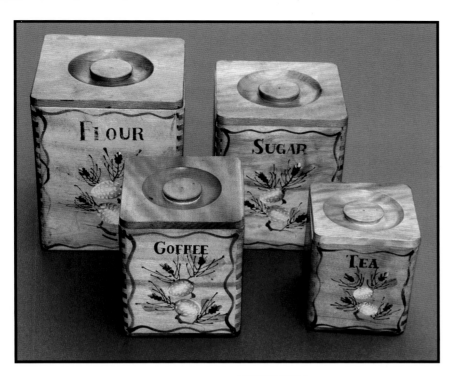

Left:
More recent wood canisters also decorated with pinecone designs. This set probably dates from the 1960s and the maker is unknown. (Set, $20).

Set of vintage pinecone decorated wood salad bowls. The only marks are on the bottom of the bowls: "G G 20-C E" and "G G 2/M." Part of the design is burned while the rest appears to be hand painted. (Set $20+).

Unmarked metal pinecone tray circa 1960s. This is one of a set of four trays, probably produced when TV trays were so popular. These trays could still be used when transferring food to decks or porches. ($5-$8 each).

Cocktail shaker and matching glass, circa 1950s. Several different designs of these glasses were made featuring a variety of geese or ducks. The glasses and matching accessories are especially appealing for use in cabins near lakes which are populated with these kinds of water fowl. (Glass, $4; cocktail shaker, $20).

Set of six glasses featuring a different water fowl design. (Set of six without holder, $20-$25).

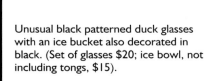

Unusual black patterned duck glasses with an ice bucket also decorated in black. (Set of glasses $20; ice bowl, not including tongs, $15).

Pitcher and matching juice size glasses in yet another water fowl design. The pitchers are harder to find than the various glasses. *Courtesy of Avalanche Ranch, Redstone, Colorado.*

For a cabin near the ski slopes, glasses which feature skiers on both sides would make interesting kitchen accessories, as they could be for display or for use. ($6 each).

Another set of glasses that would be appropriate for the winter cabin are these which feature deer and pine trees as decorations. (Set, $12-$15).

For the cabin near a lake, sailboat motifs used on kitchen products would add interest and color to a kitchen or dining area. In the 1930s, sailboats provided designs for many kitchen items including metal canister sets, McKee refrigerator dishes, and the well-known blue depression glass pieces decorated with the white sailboats. Made by the Hazel Atlas Glass Co. in the late 1930s, these items have been popular with collectors for years. The Hazel Atlas Glass Co. sailboat or ships series of Modern Tone included many different pieces: cup (plain), saucer, 8" salad plate, 5 7/8" sherbet plate, 9" dinner plate, 11 different sizes of glasses including a shot glass 2 1/2" tall, pitchers (both with and without lips), cocktail mixer, cocktail shaker, and ice bowl. (Pitcher, $55-$65; glasses, $13-$15 each.)

Ice bowl and two smaller scaled glasses also produced by the Hazel Atlas Glass Co. in the 1930s. (Ice bucket, $35; glasses, $20 each).

Camp Blankets, Quilts, and Comforts

Stack of camp blankets featuring a variety of styles and colors. Blankets can be stacked on a shelf or in a cabinet or basket to add color to a cabin room. *Courtesy of Avalanche Ranch, Redstone, Colorado.*

Camp blankets, quilts, and comforts are both useful and decorative accessories that add splashes of color and interest to a cabin's décor. Although quilts have retained their popularity for centuries, old camp blankets and comforts have just recently gained new appeal as bedspreads or accessories.

The most sought after camp blanket designs for today's cabin owners are those with Indian or cowboy motifs. Surprisingly, in a circa 1916 Montgomery Ward advertisement for these "Indian Robes," several now familiar suggestions are given for the use of the blankets. Included are: couch cover, bedspreads, blankets, wall hanging for a den, or use on a porch. The blankets were priced from $1.59 to $4.39 each. The cheaper ones were all cotton while the expensive $4.39 examples had a wool filling and a cotton warp. Each blanket came in a variety of colors. These types of blankets continued to be advertised in mainstream mail order catalogs for decades until the 1960s. Most of the blankets were bound with sateen along the top and bottom edges and most were made of cotton until the 1940s when nylon and other synthetic fibers were blended into the fabrics.

The most collectible camp blankets are those made by the Beacon Manufacturing Co. in New Bedford, Massachusetts, and later of Swannanoa, North Carolina. Charles Owen Dexter and Charles D. Owen, I founded the firm circa 1904-05. The Owens family remained involved with the blanket business until 1969. It is hard to identify a Beacon blanket unless it carries an original label or is pictured in the *Beacon Blankets Make Warm Friends* book by Jerry and Kathy Brownstein. One of the company labels states "Beacon Blanket/Largest Manufacturer of Blankets in the World." In addition to using the Beacon materials for blankets, other firms purchased the goods from the company to produce "blanket" bathrobes. These products were also made for decades. The most popular were designed for men and boys. When hung on a bathroom door or a rustic coat rack in a bedroom, such robes add a touch of nostalgia to a cabin setting.

Other blankets sought for cabin decorating include those produced by the Hudson's Bay Co. in England. The wool blankets have been made for centuries and were created to be used for trade with the American Indians circa 1779. The stripes, or points, represent the number of beaver pelts a blanket brought. The Montgomery Ward Fall and Winter catalog for 1959 advertised the company's blankets for $30.95 each. Buyers had a choice of the traditional white with multi-stripe border, or green or red with a black stripe. Because the blankets were expensive for the average household, other United States firms produced their own versions of the blankets. This same catalog offered a U.S. copy of the famous blanket for $15.98, a savings of $15.00 for the buyer. Today's collectors need to be sure they are purchasing a real Hudson Bay blanket by checking the label.

There are many ways camp blankets can be used in decorating a cabin. A variety of the colorful blankets can be stacked on a shelf, in a cabinet, or even on a sled to allow the various designs and colors of the blankets to show. Blankets hanging on pegs in an entryway or mud room will add color accents to an otherwise uninteresting area. A backpack or other basket can be filled with rolled or folded blankets and placed beside a fireplace or used to enhance a fishing or hunting wall arrangement. If a collector is lucky enough to find a blanket that blends with bedding, it can be hung on a wall or folded at the foot of a bed to make a more interesting bed covering. "Cutters" (blankets too worn to be displayed full size) should never be thrown away. The remaining material still in good condition can be made into throw pillows to be used on a bed, couch, or chair. In addition, camp blankets brighten any corner of a cabin when placed over the back of a chair, couch, or table.

Camp blanket prices will vary according to maker, condition, design, color, and material. The most expensive blankets are those featuring a "Beacon" label designed with an Indian motif, and in excellent condition. Blankets with nylon or other synthetic fibers are newer and, therefore, cheaper in price. Blankets that have "balled" or that contain large holes or thin worn places are the least expensive. In between are the blankets that are in relatively good shape, perhaps missing parts of their binding or with a small tear or two. Even blanket pillows need to be made of strong material, so the buyer should look the blanket over carefully before making a purchase. If a blanket is to be hung on a peg as part of a display, a less expensive blanket will work nicely.

Quilts have also gained additional popularity as a decorating tool in the last twenty years or so. At first, this interest in quilts was driven by popularity of the "country" look, but currently both cottage and cabin décor can be enhanced by incorporating quilts into their decorating schemes. Even though vintage quilts are still primarily used on beds, pillows and a camp blanket can be combined with the quilt to add a new look. Baskets and vintage quilt racks can also be used to display quilts in a bedroom or by a fireplace. If a quilt contains the proper colors and is not too large, it can be used as a table covering, particularly for a special arrangement such as Christmas. Very unusual quilts can also be used as wall hangings if space allows. Even though there are so many new imported quilts on the market, the vintage handmade quilts still offer the nicest cabin look. For those lucky enough to own quilts made by family members, cabins offer a wonderful place for their use and display.

In addition to quilts, handmade comforts, usually made of dark materials, have recently become collectible. As late as the 1970s, these bulky covers could be purchased at farm auctions for $3.00 to $5.00 each. Today, those same covers are bringing as much as $50 or more. Most of these comforts were made with squares of heavy material, often wool, sewed into a top which was then combined with a batting and usually a flannel backing. Because the comfort was so heavy it could not be quilted, so it was tied together with yarn in most of the squares. Due to the lack of heat in many homes during the early part of the twentieth century, particularly in the upstairs bedrooms, these heavy comforts were used a great deal during cold winter nights. Unlike quilts, these covers, as a rule, were not works of art; rather, they were made as necessities. In today's cabin, a comfort can be folded at the foot of a bed, used in conjunction with a camp blanket, or utilized as a "cutter" to supply decorative pillows for any cabin room. Some of the early wool comforts were put together with a feather stitch using a crazy quilt design but most of the wool comforts were tied with yarn even when a pattern was followed. Extra special comforts can be displayed on a wall, with or without a stretcher, if enough wall space is available.

With all the ways camp blankets, quilts, and comforts can be used in decorating today's cabin, it's certain that bedding is not just for bedding any more.

Camp blankets or "Indian Blankets" as they used to be called, were advertised in the mail order catalogs from the early 1900s until the early 1960s. This ad from a Montgomery Ward catalog is circa 1916. It featured three blankets priced from $1.59 to $4.39 each. The cheaper examples were made of cotton while the more expensive one had a wool filling and a cotton wrap. Suggestions for use of the blankets included: bedspread, couch cover, den wall hanging, or for the porch.

Left:
"Indian" type blankets were pictured in color in the Sears Fall and Winter catalog for 1931-1932. The blanket with the Indian design was priced at $2.59. It was made of China cotton and a small amount of wool. A larger size of the same blanket cost $2.98. A "Broken Block Plaid" designed blanket was also pictured and sold for the same price.

A variety of Indian blankets were pictured in the Sears Fall and Winter catalog of 1935-1936. Several designs were featured in prices ranging from $1.00 to $1.98 each. All of the blankets were woven of American and imported cotton. The most expensive blanket was finished with a sateen binding.

The Montgomery Ward Christmas catalog of 1934 also advertised "Indian Design Blankets." The blankets were made of American and curly China cotton. The catalog copy read "Smooth suede finish and sateen bound edges." The blanket was priced at $1.49 and was offered in four colors as pictured.

The Spiegel Fall and Winter catalog from 1944 pictured one Indian styled blanket that came in three different color combinations. It was made of "American and imported cotton yarns." Suggestions for uses included: couch throw, for a boy's room or den, and for camping trips. It sold for $2.09.

Beacon labeled "Indian" blanket displayed in a vintage "gathering basket." The label reads "Beacon Blanket/$2.29/Largest Manufacturer of Blankets in the World/Rayon and Nylon/Mohawk/54" x 72". The Beacon firm began the practice of blending synthetic fibers into its fabrics in the late 1940s. (Blanket $115-$125; basket, $98). *Courtesy of Avalanche Ranch, Redstone, Colorado.*

The "Indian" styled blankets were still being featured in the Montgomery Ward Fall and Winter catalog for 1955-1956. Item #K was called an "Apache" blanket and #M was titled "Iroquois." The blankets were no longer produced in cotton but were made of 90 percent rayon and 10 percent nylon. The larger "Apache" sold for $3.39 and "Iroquois" was priced at $2.39. The "Apache" design blanket still remained in the Montgomery Ward catalog in 1960.

Men's bathrobes were made from Beacon cloth for many decades of the 20th century. Although the early garments were produced of cotton or wool, the later examples contained synthetic materials mixed with the cotton. The Montgomery Ward Fall and Winter catalog for 1959 sold a "Beacon Cloth" men's robe which was made of a blend of acetate and cotton. It came in blue, maroon, or grey and was priced at $8.98.

Soft, Warm Beacon Cloth $7.47

Sells Nationally for $8.95. Brent Robe of 55% Acetate, 45% Cotton. Rayon cord trim and belt. Double shawl collar. 3 pockets. Dry clean. Ship. wt. 2 lbs. 6 oz. *State size, color.*

Reg. Sizes: Small (34-36); Med. (37-40 in.); Large (41-44); Ex. Large (46-48 in. chests). 35A4850—Blue, Maroon, Charcoal Gray. $7.47

Tall Size: Men 6 ft. or over. Fits 40-42. 35 A 4851—Blue or Maroon..........$8.98

ALL WARDS 491

Never-used Beacon labeled blanket 66" x 80" in size. In their book, *Beacon Blankets Make Warm Friends,* the Brownsteins refer to this label as being used on "New, Old Stock." The label reads "BEACON BLANKETS MAKE WARM FRIENDS." No fabric content is listed. Both ends are finished with sateen binding. ($115-$125).

Beacon cloth men's robe similar to the one pictured in the 1959 Montgomery Ward catalog. The label reads "65% ACETATE – 35% COTTON/GENUINE/BEACON/FABRIC." These vintage robes can be hung on a hook on the back of a bathroom door or on a coat rack in a bedroom. ($30+).

The Montgomery Ward Fall and Winter catalog for 1959 advertised Hudson's Bay wool blankets in three colors. The famous blankets, made in Great Britain, have been produced for centuries and are still being made today. Catalog information states that the "blankets were guaranteed mothproof for life." The blankets were offered in white with a multi-striped border, and green or red with a black stripe. The blankets sold for $30.95 each. Currently new blankets in a twin size are priced at approximately $200 and the full size at $300. *(See text for more information).*

Vintage Hudson's Bay off-white wool blanket with the multi-striped design in a double bed size. This design has always been the most popular of the Hudson's Bay products. The blankets have been best sellers for L.L. Bean since 1925. Their advertising states that the blankets are both "wind and water proof." ($300). *Courtesy of Avalanche Ranch, Redstone, Colorado.*

The Hudson's Bay Company label identified their original blankets. Many other firms produced "look alike" wool blankets that were priced at approximately half of the cost of the Hudson's Bay blankets. The label reads "ALL GENUINE HUDSON'S BAY POINT BLANKETS BEARS THIS SEAL/ HUDSON'S BAY COMPANY/ INCORPORATED 1670/THE SEAL OF QUALITY/MADE IN ENGLAND." *Courtesy of Avalanche Ranch, Redstone, Colorado.*

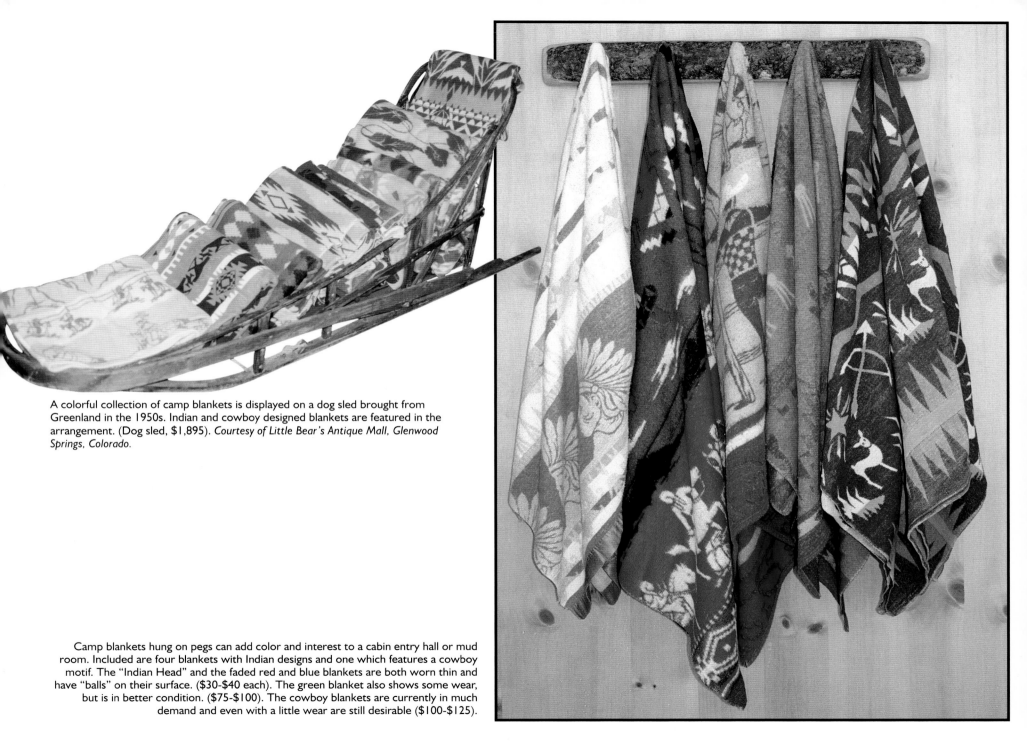

A colorful collection of camp blankets is displayed on a dog sled brought from Greenland in the 1950s. Indian and cowboy designed blankets are featured in the arrangement. (Dog sled, $1,895). *Courtesy of Little Bear's Antique Mall, Glenwood Springs, Colorado.*

Camp blankets hung on pegs can add color and interest to a cabin entry hall or mud room. Included are four blankets with Indian designs and one which features a cowboy motif. The "Indian Head" and the faded red and blue blankets are both worn thin and have "balls" on their surface. ($30-$40 each). The green blanket also shows some wear, but is in better condition. ($75-$100). The cowboy blankets are currently in much demand and even with a little wear are still desirable ($100-$125).

Camp blankets can be rolled tightly and placed in vintage pack baskets to make an interesting display to be used beside a fireplace. The brown blanket with the multi-colored stripes is wool ($35-$50), the excellent brown and cream blanket is bound with sateen on both ends ($125+); and the small blanket is a "cutter" and is no longer a full blanket.

Camp blankets can also be used as wall hangings when appropriate colors can be found. This blanket is in very good condition and blends well with a new quilted bedspread. (Blanket, $100+).

A brown and cream vintage camp blanket is highlighted with the use of a new lamp which features a stained glass shade. It sits on an old wicker table. An unfinished piece of embroidery work is also pictured. (Blanket in excellent condition, $125+).

This cozy corner is given needed color with the addition of a vintage camp blanket chosen to blend with the collection of Colorado yellow Coors pottery and the brown oak church pew. Two hand-embroidered pillows also add interest to the arrangement. (Coors pottery, $50-$100 each; blanket in very good condition, $75+; pine cone pillow, $75+; flowered pillow, $40+).

New Old Hickory queen-sized bed fitted with a modern quilted off-white bedspread, pillows made from a vintage camp blanket and featuring an old wool blanket folded across its foot. Even though most collectors prefer the vintage Old Hickory products, beds offer a real challenge. If examples can be found at all, they are not large enough to satisfy most people who prefer queen or king size beds. The new beds are quite attractive and fit nicely with the old pieces of Indiana hickory furniture. (Pillows, $20+ each; blanket, $35+).

The co-author's baby bassinet, now over seventy years old, has been filled with a collection of camp blankets so they can be displayed in a bedroom window seat. Although the basket was originally cream in color, it was repainted nearly fifty years ago for a new baby's arrival. The blue has aged nicely to blend with the vintage blankets.

A vintage handmade blue and yellow quilt sets the tone for this bedroom setting. The colors are repeated with the use of a wool blanket which features stripes in a matching blue and yellow. Hand embroidered pillows decorate the head of the antique brass bed. An old brass Rayo lamp, which has been electrified, sits on a rustic table decorated with pyrographic frames. The bed and lamp are circa 1915-1925, the frames date from the early 1900s, vintage pillows are from 1915 to 1930s, and the quilt is circa 1940s. The blanket is of more recent vintage and carries a J.C. Penny label. (Brass bed, $200+; mint condition quilt, $250+; lamp, $80; blanket, $25; pillows $20-$50 each, depending on size, age and design).

Interesting curtain made from a vintage camp blanket. A bamboo ski pole acts as a curtain rod. Camp blankets could also be used to fashion drapes in a cabin home. *Courtesy of Avalanche Ranch, Redstone, Colorado.*

Quilts can also be displayed as wall hangings, over banisters, or on quilt racks. These two simple family quilts date from the 1930s. They are displayed on a vintage wood quilt rack circa 1920s. The framed calendar dates from 1937. It advertises Rees Lumber and Hardware Co. located in Burlington Junction, Missouri. (Quilts with some wear, $50-$75 each; quilt rack, $50+; framed calendar, $35-$45).

Souvenir rayon and satin pillows dominate this bedroom setting suitable for cabin use. The pastel quilt was pieced by the co-author in the 1950s and quilted by her grandmother. Pillow tops like the ones pictured were sold as souvenirs from the World War I years through the 1950s. Pillows used on this bed represent states, cities, and tourist destinations. They include Colorado, California, Kansas City, Missouri, Wind Cave National Park, South Dakota, and Franconia Notch, New Hampshire. An Indian camp blanket featuring the pastel colors of the quilt has been folded across vintage metal bed circa 1920-1925 painted white. (Quilt with some fading on corner, $75-$100; pillow covers, $10-$15 each; bed, $50).

When the top of this "Star" quilt from the 1940s is folded, the vintage hand embroidered sheets and pillow cases used on the bed are allowed to show. This kind of an arrangement can be used with any simple quilt or bedspread. Although the old embroidered pillow cases are still readily available, the embroidered sheets are harder to come by. An antique brass bed is in keeping with the vintage bedding. (Bed, $200+; quilt, $250+; embroidered pillow cases, $15-$25 set; embroidered sheets, $25-$45 each).

45

Besides beds, quilts can also be used as table coverings provided the size is right. This red and green circa 1940s example has only been used during Christmas celebrations. It fits nicely over a large oak conference table now used as a dining table. A small old Christmas tree, decorated with antique and vintage ornaments occupies the center of the table. Other items displayed include a Christmas box, two cardboard and paper Santas by Beistle, Christmas tree fence also by Beistle, celluloid Santa, candle sticks, and a "Dennison's Christmas Book" from 1921. (Quilt, $75-$100; tree, $45; other items $25-$50 each).

Opposite page, bottom left:
This vintage "crazy quilt" falls somewhere between the quilt and comfort category. Most of these types of quilts included pieces made of satin and other materials that rotted with age. Because of that, it is hard to find one of these examples in excellent condition. This one, however, is made of wool and sateen fabrics. It remains in fine condition. The pieces have been feather stitched together so that the gold stitching becomes part of the design. Blue, black, and dark rose pieces dominate the color scheme. The finished top, inside batting, and backing were tied together with yarn since the materials were too thick to be quilted. Because of the fabric and colors used in this quilt, it could also add to a cabin's décor when used on a bed, wall, or stair railing. A vintage hand embroidered pillow is also pictured. (Comfort, $50+; pillow, $30+).

Opposite page, right:
Another more traditional old wool comfort has been mounted on stretchers and hung on a bedroom wall. This keeps the comfort from sagging and makes for a nicer display. Like most vintage comforts, this one uses squares of wool in its design with red, navy blue, black, and green as its predominate colors. The colors of the comfort blend nicely with the modern bedspread. Hand embroidered pillows and a vintage crocheted throw add interest to the antique sleigh bed. Two pieces of the owner's pottery collection are shown on the bedside table. *Private Collection.* (Comfort, $55-$75).

Below:
This family comfort was made in the early 1950s, using scraps of corduroy. It is pictured on a mission style oak bed, circa 1910. Red pillow cases, plaid pillows made from a vintage Pendleton robe, and a hand decorated denim fabric pillow add interest to the tall headboard. A vintage red wool blanket has been folded across the foot of the bed. It was made by the Minnesota Woolen Co. in Duluth, Minnesota, circa 1950s. Black stitching around the edges and a black stripe decorate the blanket. An old wood lamp (with a new "Colorado" shade), a souvenir covered wagon, and a vintage radio share space on the top of an antique oak sewing machine cabinet. (Bed, $200+; sewing machine cabinet, $125; radio, $40; blanket, $15-$20; comfort, $35-$50; pillows, $10-$30 each).

Rustic and Casual Cabin Furniture

With the prosperity of the 1990s, more and more people began building second homes to use for weekend getaways or during vacation breaks. Many of these structures were cabins or cottages built near water, mountains, or in warm climates. Also on the upswing in the 1990s' building boom were structures made of logs, both for year-round living and for use as weekend retreats. Because these new buildings needed unique furnishings, a revival of interest in the old rustic furniture occurred. Such pieces fit perfectly in the new as well as the old log homes and cabins. Not only has this new interest raised prices on the old twig, root, log, and hickory furniture, the appeal has sparked many new businesses which now reproduce these types of furnishings as well as the accompanying accessories.

In addition to the furniture termed "rustic," other types of furniture can be mixed with these pieces to give a more integrated look to a cabin's decor. Both wicker and Mission oak furnishings were used in the early Adirondack camps and they are still appropriate cabin furnishings today.

Indiana Hickory and Other Rustic Furniture

Some of the most popular old pieces that can be found today are those made by several firms in Indiana that once produced various styles of hickory furniture during much of the twentieth century.

The most prolific of these firms began business in Martinsville, Indiana, under the name "Old Hickory Chair Co.," circa 1894. According to Joanne Raetz Stuttgen in her book *Martinsville A Pictorial History*, the local newspaper printed an announcement on May 10, 1894 that George F. Richardson from Indianapolis had opened the Old Hickory Chair Factory in the former Christian Church building. According to Stuttgen, the firm moved to a larger Martinsville facility in 1900 and, with later expansion, remained in that factory until closure in 1978. After several changes in ownership, the company was purchased by William H. Patton in 1908. Under Patton's leadership, according to an article in the *Martinsville Republican* for Feb. 8, 1921, the directors changed the name of the firm to the Old Hickory Furniture Co. "to enter a wider field in the furniture manufacturing world."

Even during the early years, the firm offered nearly one hundred different items for sale, including chairs, rockers, tables, toy furniture, benches, office furniture, "tête a tête" chairs, foot stools, settees, couches, park and hotel seats, cradles, cradles connected to a rocking chair, library tables, porch swings, planters, rustic bridges, summer houses, log houses, and walking sticks. Many pieces of this furniture were used to furnish National Park inns and lodges throughout the country. Some of these original pieces are still in place today.

As the years passed, many of the original designs continued to be sold by the company for decades. In addition, more modern examples of the hickory furniture were also produced. In the 1930s, upholstered furniture as well as butterfly tables, ladderback chairs, and other more modern designs had been added to the line. By the 1940s, because of the shortage of materials during World War II, many pieces were being designed with cushions or canvas backs and seats. According to Craig Gilborn, writing in *Adirondack Furniture and the Rustic Tradition,* in the later years of production, nylon webbing was used for the backs and seats of many of the hickory chairs.

The Patton family retained ownership of the company until after Charles Patton's death in 1965, when the Old Hickory Furniture Co. was sold to the Aquamarine Corp. of Cleveland, Ohio. After this sale, the output of the well-known rustic furniture company changed dramatically. In 1968, both the Old Hickory firm, as well as Aquamarine, its parent company, had been merged with Ramada Inns. According to an article from the *Martinsville Daily Reporter* dated Dec. 10, 1968, James Banfield, the general manager of the Old Hickory firm, announced that most of the furniture produced in the local plant would be used by Ramada Inns throughout the country.

One of the new innovations at the plant included the production of barrel furniture, which had been done on a lesser scale beginning in the late 1930s. In an article that appeared in the Bloomington, Indiana *Sunday Tribune and Star Courier* for August 17, 1969, the line of furniture was listed as including barrel chairs of several styles, stools, convertible tables, bars, coffee and end tables. The pieces were to be used mostly in game or family rooms. The furniture was upholstered in Naugahyde.

The Old Hickory factory returned to local ownership in 1970, when brothers John and Ralph Miles purchased the company. According to an article in the *Martinsville Daily Reporter* dated Jan. 23, 1970, the pair bought the firm from Ramada Inns of Phoenix. Even with the added production of white oak barrels (*Martinsville Daily Reporter*, Nov. 9, 1970) the Miles brothers' ownership of "Old Hickory" lasted only a couple of years. The *Martinsville Daily Reporter* reported on Jan. 7, 1972 that the Ramada Development Co., a subsidiary of Ramada Inns, Inc., had re-acquired the Old Hickory Furniture Co. At that time, Ramada Inn's director of purchasing announced that the firm was placing a $300,000 order for motel furniture to be produced by the Old Hickory Company.

The *Daily Reporter* again carried an article on a change of ownership for the Old Hickory plant in December 1976. Ralph Canino, Don Elbert, and Ken Asam had entered into an agreement with Ramada Inn to purchase the plant, effective Jan. 1, 1977.

With the end of the Patton family's longtime ownership in the mid 1960s, Old Hickory Furniture Co. seemed to have lost its focus. Several changes of management pulled the firm in different directions and the long history of the company ended when the plant was closed in July 1978.

After several years, Old Hickory furniture was revived when a new owner bought the name and designs in or around 1982 and moved the company to a plant in Shelbyville, Indiana. It now manufactures many of the original furniture pieces as well as new designs to fit modern times.

The second most popular Indiana hickory furniture maker was the Rustic Hickory Furniture Co., of LaPorte, Indiana. This firm was established in 1902 by Ed Handley. It closed during the depression, circa 1933. The firm's 1904 catalog, reprinted in the book *Rustic Hickory Furniture Co. Porch, Lawn and Cottage Furniture*, edited by Victor M. Linoff, quotes very reasonable prices – from $1.20 for a child's chair to $25 for a settee and couch combination piece. Many of the items pictured are similar to the Old Hickory products but there are some different designs, including a chair with a hickory "stick" seat and back, and a rustic bench and swing, both made of hickory poles.

The 1926 "Rustic Hickory" catalog, also pictured in the Linoff book, shows many similar designs from the 1904 line with the addition of an oak dresser with hickory trim as well as hickory beds and day beds. Oak and hickory desks and library tables were also new designs. In addition, a variety of planters and a grandfather clock were added to the line.

The Indiana Willow Products Company was another Martinsville, Indiana firm that produced hickory furniture. This company was established much later, however. The firm was incorporated in 1937 by two former employees of the famous Old Hickory Furniture Co.: Clyde C. Hatley and Emerson D. Laughner. Although the "Willow" name indicates the products were to be constructed of willow, a later change to hickory was made. Many of the new company products were similar to those made by the Old Hickory Co. The firm made chairs, rockers, settees, tables, porch swings, gliders, beds (including bunk), night stands, floor lamps, table lamps, vanities, benches, stools, book racks, mirrors, dressers, chests, luggage stands, magazine racks, children's rockers, doll chairs, doll rockers and doll settees, and firewood baskets. Unlike most other firms, the Willow company also produced several styles of bars and bar stools, as well as picnic tables and benches. Instead of changing with the times, as the Old Hickory Furniture Co. did, the Willow firm pretty much stayed with older products that had been successful.

According to Joanne Raetz Stuttgen, writing in her book *Martinsville A Pictorial History*, the firm changed its name to the Indiana Hickory Furniture Co., Inc. in 1950. With changing times and styles and a loss of business, the firm ceased production in 1963.

In addition to the commercial companies producing hickory furniture in Indiana, the state itself was also involved in this industry. Beginning in 1918,

Rustic accents can add style and interest to a cabin's interior. This is an unidentified Indiana hickory settee with curved back. Rustic Hickory Furniture Co. pictured a similar piece in its 1926 catalog. Both examples feature three vertical posts on the back and double spindles around the bottom. ($600 with wear).

hickory furniture was manufactured at the state prison in Putnamville and is still being produced by Indiana inmates today. The furniture that was made by the state included tables, chairs, beds, chaise lounges, leanback chairs (some with attached foot stools), foot stools, benches, settees, gliders, counter stools, swings, and high chairs. The furniture was also used to furnish Indiana state parks, fire stations, jails, and shelter houses for decades. This rustic furniture was marketed through the use of catalogs for many years.

According to a spokesman for the Industry Division of the Indiana Department of Corrections, the furniture is now offered through a commercial firm called Rustic Integrity. Some of the current pieces include beds, chairs, rocking chairs, coffee tables, dining room tables, loveseats, lounge chairs, sofas, case goods (any furniture with drawers), and wardrobes, plus children's tables, chairs, and rockers. The furniture is finished with cane, upholstery, or leather.

Besides the more available Indiana hickory pieces, other rustic furniture was made in many parts of the United States and would be appropriate to use for cabin furnishings. Included is the stick furniture particularly popular in the Adirondacks. The best-known maker of this type of furniture is Ernest Stowe. According to Craig Gilborn writing in *Adirondack Furniture and the Rustic Tradition*, Stowe worked mostly in the Saranac Lake area making rustic furnishings for the camps then being built in the early 1900s. Most of the furniture was made from yellow birch rounds decorated with applied white birch bark. He also occasionally worked with cedar. Stowe was a master of the "applied bark" type of rustic furniture. He was a fine craftsman and with his attention to detail and unique decoration, his pieces are rare and very much in demand by today's collectors. Furniture identified as Stowe originals include chairs, tables, sideboards, arm chairs, dressers, secretaries, bookcases, desks, and decorated wall pieces to hold mirrors or clocks. Surprisingly, by all known accounts, Stowe left the Adirondacks in 1911 and moved to Florida. It is not known if he continued to produce any furniture while living in that region.

Other fine craftsmen were making rustic type furnishings in other parts of the United States as well. One of the best was Ben Davis, a Baptist circuit minister living in North Carolina. Most of his pieces were made in the 1920s and 1930s. His designs were so unique that some craftsmen are now reproducing his pieces. Davis worked mostly with rhododendron and laurel roots, twigs, and branches. All of the Reverend's furniture was heavily decorated and beautifully done. His pieces

are very rare so they are hard to find and expensive to purchase. Ann Stillman O'Leary pictures one of his pieces in her book *Adirondack Style*, published in 1998.

Root and burl furniture was also appreciated by the early Adirondack camp owners. Tables with root bases and burl tops were especially desirable.

Other interesting innovations used to decorate rustic furniture include "mosaic twig" work. With this method, prepared twigs are applied to a piece of furniture following a design already drawn on the project. New as well as old pieces of this type of furni-

Old Hickory Chair advertisement appeared in the Good Housekeeping magazine circa 1910. The "Andrew Jackson" hoop chair pictured had escalated in price to $3.50. A rustic three-legged table was also shown selling for $8.00. The ad copy stated that the Old Hickory furniture had been used in furnishing "Claremont-on-the-Hudson, Old Faithful Inn, and the West Baden Hotel." A customer could write for a catalog "showing 150 types of Old Hickory."

Advertisement for the Old Hickory Chair Co. which appeared in *McClures* magazine in the early 1900s. The Martinsville, Indiana firm produced rustic hickory furniture from around 1894 until the 1960s. The name and production were revived in the mid-1980s in a new location in Shelbyville, Indiana.

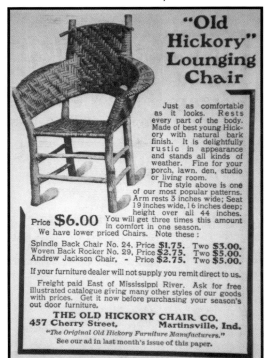

ture can be purchased by today's collector.

Thomas C. Molesworth (1890-1977), a furniture maker from Cody, Wyoming, produced rustic furniture with a western appeal. He worked with wood, leather, antlers, Indian weavings, fringe, and bright colors to complete his pieces. (*See The Western Look chapter*.)

Wood furniture made of peeled logs has also remained popular for many years. This material is especially appealing for beds. Well-known furniture stores have carried these types of products for a decade or more. Of course, the old examples are always the most desirable.

Less popular rustic furniture has also been constructed using animal horns or antlers. Chairs and stools made with steer horns as well as chairs, beds, and tables decorated with antlers are all examples of these types of furniture. More popular are the lamps and light fixtures made with shed antlers.

Montgomery Ward catalog ad circa 1916 which pictures "Genuine Old Hickory Furniture." Montgomery Ward may have contracted with the Old Hickory firm to produce several of these designs just for Montgomery Ward to be sold in their catalog. The copy reads "these pieces are built of hickory, the strongest of the native woods. The bottoms and backs are plaited by hand of the inner growth hickory bark which is stripped from the tree. Hickory bark is of far greater strength than any other seating material and for this reason, these pieces will last almost a life time." The most inexpensive chair was priced at $2.75 and the highest priced item shown was the swing for $8.65.

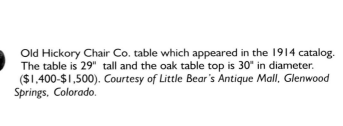

Old Hickory Chair Company ad in the *Good Housekeeping* magazine for May 1916. Pictured and priced are a three-piece "Andrew Jackson" set including a rocker, chair, and table priced at $16.75 and a cheaper three-piece set in a different design that sold for only $13.75.

Old Hickory Chair Co. table which appeared in the 1914 catalog. The table is 29" tall and the oak table top is 30" in diameter. ($1,400-$1,500). *Courtesy of Little Bear's Antique Mall, Glenwood Springs, Colorado.*

The branded mark on the sewing rocker reads "OLD HICKORY/ CHAIR CO./MARTINSVILLE, IND." *Scott collection.*

Right:
The Old Hickory sewing rocker still retains its original paper label. The label includes the following information: "OLD HICKORY/HIGHGRADE/ RUSTIC FURNITURE/BOOKLET SHOWING INDUSTRIAL DESIGN FOR THE ASKING/ANDREW JACKSON CHAIR/OLD HICKORY CHAIR CO./MARTINSVILLE, IND." *Scott collection.*

Small Old Hickory sewing rocker branded "OLD HICKORY CHAIR CO. MARTINSVILLE, IND." This mark was used until the company made its name change to Old Hickory Furniture Co. in 1921. This chair is circa 1919-1920 and has its original paper label. The old fishing creel beside the chair is being used as a sewing basket. ($600+ with paper label.) *From the collection of Bob Scott.*

Old Hickory armchair with distinctive decoration across the back. It is also branded "OLD HICKORY/CHAIR CO./MARTINSVILLE, IND." The seat on this chair has been re-caned. It is circa 1919-1920. ($550+ with replaced seat.) *Scott collection.*

Old Hickory porch swing, one of two originally purchased for Grand Lake Lodge in Grand Lake, Colorado, circa 1919-20, along with many other Old Hickory pieces used to furnish the lodge when it opened in 1920. The seat has been replaced, but the swing is still used on the front porch of the lodge's "Honeymoon" cabin. The swing is marked with the early "OLD HICKORY/CHAIR CO." trademark. The upper back of the swing matches the decoration on the back of the armchair pictured earlier. ($1,000+ with replaced seat.) *Courtesy of Grand Lake Lodge, Grand Lake, Colorado.*

This 1937 postcard pictures the Old Hickory swing in its original position on the porch at Grand Lake Lodge. Two matching swings were placed on the porch when the lodge opened in 1920. By 1937, directors chairs provided most of the seating for the porch area.

Another original Old Hickory piece from the Grand Lake Lodge is this square table that includes a checker board design on its oak top. The circa 1919-1920 table is still used by patrons in the establishment's bar. It is likely that the table came complete with the checker board decoration but it has not been verified by a catalog illustration. (Not enough examples to determine a price.) *Courtesy of Grand Lake Lodge, Grand Lake, Colorado.*

Old Hickory straight chair circa 1919-1920 that retains part of its original paper label. The chair also includes the brand "OLD HICKORY CHAIR CO./ MARTINSVILLE, IND." ($450+). *From the collection of Bob Scott.*

Old Hickory rocker circa 1919-1920 that now features the hide of a Longhorn steer on the back and seat instead of the original hickory bark. It, too, carries the burned in "OLD HICKORY CHAIR CO./MARTINSVILLE, IND." mark. ($550+ with replaced seat and back). *From the collection of Bob Scott.*

This matching Old Hickory settee also dates from 1919-1920. The seat has been replaced. It carries the original "OLD HICKORY CHAIR CO./MARTINSVILLE, IND." mark. A similar piece was pictured in a Belknap Hardware and Manufacturing Co. catalog circa 1920s. It measures 34.5" tall x 39.5" wide x 18.5" x deep. ($1,000+ with replaced seat.) *Scott collection.*

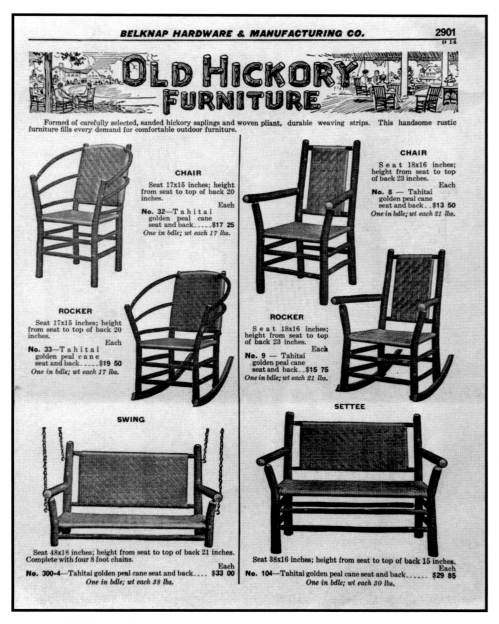

OLD HICKORY FURNITURE

Formed of carefully selected, sanded hickory saplings and woven pliant, durable weaving strips. This handsome rustic furniture fills every demand for comfortable outdoor furniture.

CHAIR

Seat 17x15 inches; height from seat to top of back 20 inches.
Each
No. 32—Tahitai golden peal cane seat and back.....**$17 25**
One in bdle; wt each 17 lbs.

CHAIR

Seat 18x16 inches; height from seat to top of back 23 inches.
Each
No. 8 — Tahitai golden peal cane seat and back..**$13 50**
One in bdle; wt each 21 lbs.

ROCKER

Seat 17x15 inches; height from seat to top of back 20 inches.
Each
No. 33—Tahitai golden peal cane seat and back.....**$19 50**
One in bdle; wt each 17 lbs.

ROCKER

Seat 18x16 inches; height from seat to top of back 23 inches.
Each
No. 9 — Tahitai golden peal cane seat and back..**$15 75**
One in bdle; wt each 21 lbs.

SWING

Seat 48x18 inches; height from seat to top of back 21 inches.
Complete with four 8 foot chains.
Each
No. 300-4—Tahitai golden peal cane seat and back.....**$33 00**
One in bdle; wt each 38 lbs.

SETTEE

Seat 38x16 inches; height from seat to top of back 15 inches.
Each
No. 104—Tahitai golden peal cane seat and back......**$29 85**
One in bdle; wt each 30 lbs.

OLD HICKORY FURNITURE

"Old Hickory" for many years has proven much in demand because of its sturdiness and attractive rustic appearance. Formed of carefully selected, sanded hickory saplings and woven pliant, durable weaving strips.

CHAIR

Seat 18x16 inches; height from seat to top of back 22 inches.
Each
No. 24 — Tahitai golden peal cane seat......**$10 20**
Two in bdle; wt each 21 lbs.

CHAIR

Seat 18x16 inches; height from seat to top of back 20 inches.
Each
No. N20 — Tahitai golden peal cane seat......**$9 45**
Two in bdle; wt each 20 lbs.

ROCKER

Seat 18x16 inches; height from seat to top of back 22 inches.
Each
No. 25— Tahitai golden peal cane seat.....**$12 60**
Two in bdle; wt each 21 lbs.

ROCKER

Seat 18x16 inches; height from seat to top of back 20 inches.
Tahitai golden peal cane seat.
No.............**N21**
Each............**$12 00**
Two in bdle; wt each 21 lbs.

TABLE

Each
No. 198—Round oak top 30 inches in diameter; height over all 30 inches....**$34 50**
One in bdle; wt each 40 lbs.

SETTEE—Seat 38x16 inches; height back 18 inches.   Each
No. 110—Tahitai golden peal seat; wt 34 lbs..........**$23 25**

SWING—Seat 48x18 ins; height back 20 inches.   Each
No. 264—Tahitai golden peal cane seat; wt 36 lbs.....**$23 25**

Later Old Hickory furniture featured in a Belknap Hardware and Manufacturing Co. catalog, date unknown, perhaps 1920s. This may have been a wholesale catalog and the costs quoted are supposed to represent retail prices, (sometimes inflated in vintage wholesale catalogs). The information described the seats and backs as being made of Tahitai golden peal cane. The pieces pictured were in the Old Hickory company catalogs from 1914 into the 1930s.

An additional page of the Belknap Hardware & Manufacturing Co. catalog. This furniture was also featured by Old Hickory from at least 1914 into the 1930s.

Old Hickory Company furniture brochure with unusual front page printed in color. It was from the Denver Dry Goods Co. in Denver, Colorado circa late 1920s or early 1930s. The pieces pictured include the hoop furniture set along with the simpler settee, rocker, straight chair, and matching swing plus a table.

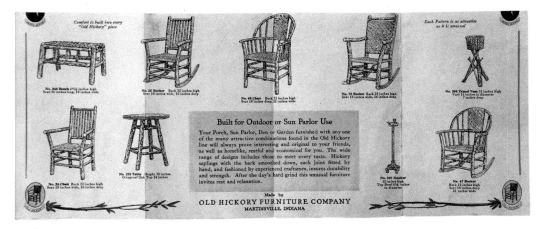

More unusual pieces were pictured in this part of the Denver Dry Goods piece. Included are a straight chair and a rocker with a captain's chair look as well as a smoker and a tripod vase.

Hickory armchair similar to one pictured in the Old Hickory catalog for 1931. The extra piece across the top of the back gives this design a little extra decoration. ($500-$600). *Courtesy Little Bear's Antique Mall, Glenwood Springs, Colorado.*

A vintage mission oak conference table, now used as a dining table, along with four matching Old Hickory side chairs and the family cat. The chairs feature an extra wood piece, sometimes called a "towel bar" across their backs. Each one is branded "Old Hickory/Martinsville/Indiana" on one of the legs. The seats and backs have been replaced. (Conference table, $1,000; set of four chairs, $1,400).

Close-up of the branded mark on the "towel bar" side chairs. It reads "Old Hickory/ Martinsville/Indiana."

"Diner" chair circa late 1930s. The chair features an open weave pattern on its back and seat which was made with rattan. ($450+). *Courtesy Avalanche Ranch, Redstone, Colorado.*

Indiana hickory chairs and table which make a nice three-piece set even though the table was made by the Old Hickory Furniture Co. and the chairs came from the Rustic Hickory Furniture Co. The table is an older model as it is branded "Old Hickory Chair Co./Martinsville Ind." Since the firm's name was changed to the "Old Hickory Furniture Co." in 1921, this table was made before that name change took place. This was a standard table design for the firm for many years. This table is shorter (26" tall) than those pictured in the catalogs, so it may have been cut down. The standard height was 28"-30". The table tops were made of oak. The matching hoop rocker and straight chair were made by the Rustic Hickory Furniture Co. in LaPorte, Indiana. This firm was established in 1902 and remained in business until 1933. Their products were identified with a pink and green paper label. Both of these chairs still carry the remains of these labels which originally read "Rustic Hickory Co./Trade Mark/LaPorte, Indiana." These two chair designs were carried in the company's catalogs for decades. Since they were purchased with the pictured table, it may indicate that they are perhaps similar in age. The Mission styled lamp is appropriate to use both with these pieces of furniture and in any cabin setting. The original stain on the oak base is very dark to match the black metal frame of the lamp shade, which features green stained glass. (Table, $500; rocker, $650; chair, $550; lamp, $250).

The Old Hickory Furniture Co. catalog for 1939 featured this page of American Provincial Chestnut Furniture. Included in the advertisement was a "Chestnut Drop Leaf Butterfly Table, Chestnut Corner Cupboard, Chestnut Server, Chestnut Welsh Dresser, Chestnut Arm Chair, and Chestnut Side Chair."

Pictured is a side chair like the one shown in the Old Hickory Furniture Co. 1939 catalog. It has a hand-woven hickory bark back. The chair is marked on the bottom "Old Hickory/Martinsville/Indiana." (One of a set of 6; $1,800-$1,900 set). *Little Bear's Antique Mall, Glenwood Springs, Colorado.*

Also pictured in the Old Hickory 1939 catalog are several rustic pieces based on earlier designs. Included are a matching settee, rocker, and armchair. New innovations included pine arm rests on all three pieces.

Mission oak library table and hickory dining chair are used together in this office cabin setting. The chair carries part of its original label from the Rustic Hickory Furniture Co. located in LaPorte, Indiana. A pair of framed Old Hickory Furniture Co. ads decorate the wall. A brass Rayo lamp and a vintage Underwood typewriter add a touch of nostalgia. See page 58 for two examples of Rustic Hickory Furniture Co. chairs. (Oak library table $200-$250; chair with replaced seat and back, $300; framed ads, $60; Rayo lamp, $75; typewriter, $40+).

The 1939 Old Hickory catalog featured several pictures in color as well as the more usual black and white photographs. The furnishings for the "ideal recreation room" are especially interesting. Included were a "Chestnut Keg Table" and four "Chestnut Keg Stools," as well as a "Chestnut Sawbuck Table and Benches." A "Chestnut Davenport" and "Chestnut Chair" with wing-like arm rests, and "Chestnut Lamp Table, Chestnut Coffee Table, Chestnut Bookend Lamp, and Chestnut Spider Floor Lamp" completed the furnishings for the room. The company continued producing a variety of contemporary lines along with some rustic furniture throughout the rest of its existence.

The Indiana Willow Products Co. Inc. of Martinsville, Indiana didn't begin business until 1937. It changed its name to the Indiana Hickory Furniture Co., Inc. in 1950 and ceased production in 1963. Their early products were marked with the label pictured here. Unlike the other earlier firms, Indiana Willow cautioned customers that the weaving in their products was fiber and was not weather resistant. "INDIANA WILLOW PRODUCTS CO., INC./ Martinsville, Indiana" completed the information on the label.

Vintage hickory chair which features its original seat and back. This style of chair was made by several of the Indiana hickory companies, including Rustic Hickory Furniture Co., Indiana Willow Products Co., Inc. and the Old Hickory firm. It is hard to find vintage chairs with their original backs and seats in excellent condition like this example. ($450+). Pictured with the chair is a tagged Beacon camp blanket ($150), a white fur rug ($295) and an English fishing creel ($95). *Courtesy of Little Bear's Antique Mall, Glenwood Springs, Colorado.*

This hickory table design was also used by more than one Indiana hickory company. Rustic Hickory Furniture Co. and Old Hickory Furniture Co. both pictured octagon tables like this in several of their catalogs. Both tables featured oak tops. The Rustic Hickory table sold for $8.50 in its 1926 catalog. ($900+). *Courtesy of Little Bear's Antique Mall, Glenwood Springs, Colorado.*

Vintage hickory arm chair and stool. The chair back and seat as well as the top of the footstool have been replaced. Both the Old Hickory Furniture Co. and the Indiana Willow Products Co. offered similar hickory chairs and stools in their catalogs in the 1930s and 1940s. (Stool, $250-$295; chair, $450-$500). *Courtesy of Little Bear's Antique Mall, Glenwood Springs, Colorado.*

Set of hickory bar stools which are marked with the Indiana Willow Products Co. labels. They are circa 1940s. The kitchen counter has been set with place settings of French Saxon pinecone dishes. (Set of 4 stools, $1,200).

"Lean back" chair that apparently was made by Indiana prison inmates at Putnamville. Two additional models were also produced including one that had no arms and another with an attached footrest. This chair is all original. (Chair, all original, $1,700). *Courtesy of Little Bear's Antique Mall, Glenwood Springs, Colorado.*

This vanity-desk was made for a motel and is marked "Oak Hill, Ranch Motel/H.B. Allen." Several of the Indiana hickory companies produced furniture for the motel industry including the Columbus Hickory Furniture Co. of Bedford, Indiana and the Old Hickory Furniture Co. which made pieces for the Ramada Inns. The top of the vanity is made of a stain resistant material. It is not known if the maple chair originally came with the vanity-desk. (Set, $900). *Courtesy of Little Bear's Antique Mall.*

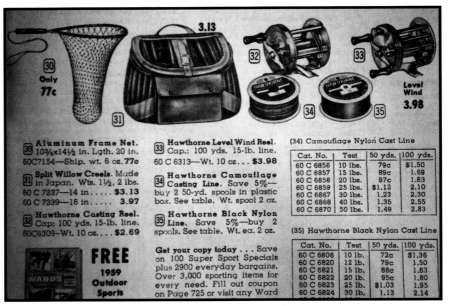

The Montgomery Ward spring and summer catalog for 1959 advertised tightly woven split willow creels "made in Japan." Both the backpack and creel in the previous picture appear to be made the same way. The newer example creel in the ad includes the addition of a snapped pocket at the front. Two sizes were offered priced at $3.13 and $3.97 depending on size. *See also Fishing chapter.*

Unidentified vintage hickory rocker with the words "Iowa State Fair" branded on the back of the chair leg. It is 37" high and 22.5" wide. The chair was one of many that were used to provide seating for patrons who attended the fair held in Des Moines each summer. The design of the chair is unusual because the front legs extend vertically above the arm pieces. In addition to the rocker, the corner is decorated with several other appropriate cabin items including a fishing net, fly rod, and fishing creel as well as a backpack which displays two examples of camp blankets. On the wall is an oak church rack which is filled with vintage maps, brochures, menus, postcards, and travel booklets. The pillow was handmade from a vintage khaki army blanket. (Rocker, $375+ with replaced seat; fishing net, $65; creel, $50; backpack, $100).

Vintage unidentified hickory rocker with the rockers set in the middle of the legs instead of on the inside of the legs as was done on most of the hickory rocking chairs of the era. The rocker features the "towel bar" design across the back. Pictured with the rocker is a fishing creel with no strap. (Rocker, $450-$500; creel, $85). *Courtesy of Little Bear's Antique Mall, Glenwood Springs, Colorado.*

Original hickory settee decorated with a "towel bar" piece across the back. The unidentified settee is one piece of a set of four. The extra embellishments across the lower front add an unusual touch. (Matching set of four pieces, $3,500+). *Courtesy of Avalanche Ranch, Redstone, Colorado.*

Left:
Hickory arm chair with a slat seat. The "Willow" firm made a similar chair but this one is unmarked. One of the advantages of these types of chairs is that the seat outwears those made of woven materials. A hand-made pillow constructed of vintage pennants adds color. The chair is pictured on one of the cabin porches of the Avalanche Ranch. (Chair, $500; pillow, $100). *Courtesy of Avalanche Ranch, Redstone, Colorado.*

Vintage hickory beds are especially interesting and, of course, much harder to find than the tables, chairs, and rockers. Several firms produced beds including the Rustic Hickory Furniture Co. which made both full and twin size models and the Indiana Willow Products Co. which marketed a bunk bed design as well as twin beds. The Old Hickory Furniture Co. offered different styles of beds through its many years in business. Although some of the designs had a rustic look, the models from the later years were more modern in design. The company sold twin, full, and in later years bunk beds in the furniture line. This unidentified hickory double bed is quite attractive with its woven designs on both the head and foot of the bed. In addition, the sides are also made with woven covering so that a quilt or camp blanket can be tucked into the bed's sides. The bed measures 51" wide x 76" long. (Bed only, $600). *Courtesy of Little Bear's Antique Mall, Glenwood Springs, Colorado.*

Child's unidentified hickory hoop rocker. Some of these types of rockers were made with three hoops. Any of the miniature or child's size hickory furniture can add an interesting decorating touch to a cabin. A vintage teddy bear occupies this chair. (Chair with some damage to the seat, $200+). *Courtesy of Avalanche Ranch, Redstone, Colorado.*

More recent lounge chair from North Carolina. Pictured with the chair is a unique Adirondack rotating twig plant stand ($350) and two camp blankets with matching colors. (Chair, $700). *Courtesy of Little Bear's Antique Mall, Glenwood Springs, Colorado.*

Vintage unidentified hickory firewood holder. Most of the companies produced this type of accessory in a variety of designs and they can be nicely displayed by a cabin fireplace or wood stove. The holders are hard to find in excellent condition because of the hard use they received. ($325). *Courtesy of Avalanche Ranch.*

Hand-crafted stick type birch rocker, circa 1950s from New England. ($495). *Courtesy of Little Bear's Antique Mall.*

Interesting couch and chairs constructed with the use of antlers. The couch pictured in the background was made with fallow deer, mule deer, and elk antlers. Deer hide was used for some of the upholstery. The chairs were constructed of mule deer antlers. (Each chair, $1,800). *Courtesy of Little Bear Antiques and Uniques, Aspen, Colorado.*

Oak hall tree utilizing antler pieces to replace the original hooks. Umbrellas, walking sticks, or canes can be stored in the bottom section. This piece would fit nicely in a cabin which features Indiana hickory or mission oak furniture or a combination of both. It now resides in a vacation home in Arkansas. ($275).

Arts and Crafts, Mission, and Wicker Furniture

A Mission oak chair, stool, and table combine with a high back Arts and Crafts wicker rocker to make a unique setting in a vacation home in Arkansas. In addition, an oak and slag glass lamp, Coors pottery, and a tall oak plant stand add interesting accessories to the grouping. The mission arm chair was made by "Lifetime," circa 1915, and the table is a Gustav Stickley product, circa 1905-1910. The stool and lamp are circa 1915 while the plant stand is from the 1920s. The chairs have been upholstered with cowhide and the wicker chair, circa 1915-1920, has been repainted. (Mission chair, $450; stool, $200; table, $1,500+; wicker chair, $400; lamp, $250+; plant stand, $175).

The most desirable Mission-Arts and Crafts furniture pieces are those produced by Gustav Stickley, the Stickley Bros. Furniture Co., L.& J.G. Stickley Company, and Charles P. Limbert & Co. from the early 1900s until shortly after the end of World War I. According to Michael Clark and Jill Thomas-Clark, writing in their book *The Stickley Brothers*, Gustav Stickley began his Gustav Stickley & Co. in Syracuse, New York in 1898. His brother's firm, the L.& J.G. Stickley Co., soon followed in 1902 and was based in Fayetteville, New York. The Stickley Bros. company was already in business in Grand Rapids, Michigan, having begun circa 1891. The last of the "big four," Charles Limbert, founded his Charles P. Limbert & Co. firm in 1902 in Grand Rapids, Michigan. Authors Michael Clark and Jill Thomas-Clark give a thorough history of all of the Stickley firms, and according to their research, by the early 1920s, all of the various Stickley companies had either ceased furniture production or changed designs to fit more modern times. These pieces are expensive, but many other examples are available which were produced by a variety of firms from the era who made cheaper, mass produced oak mission furniture.

Wicker can also work well with rustic furniture in cabin settings. This type of furniture has been popular for use on porches and in less formal rooms for decades. Many different styles of furniture have been made using a variety of materials. The Montgomery Ward catalog for 1924 features a two page spread of "fiber reed furniture" that "could be used in any room in the home," according to the advertising copy. It was especially recommended for the "sun parlor," then popular. Furniture pieces included arm chairs, rockers, settees, davenports, desks, desk chairs, six different styles of tables, chaise lounge, and a combination plant stand and bird cage. The furniture was offered plain or with upholstery. Floor and table lamps were also produced at various times but none are pictured in this ad. Advertisements in 1930s Sears mail-order catalogs stated that their furniture was "hand woven of smooth, resilient fiber." In these ads, furniture was sold in several grades and price ranges. Most of the wicker isn't marked, but a few labels have been found from Heywood Wakefield and Karpen Furniture Co. Wicker pieces are especially desirable when they include the original paint.

Newer upholstered pieces of furniture may also be necessary to ensure comfortable seating in a living room or entertainment area. Leather or colorfully covered couches or chairs are appropriate pieces to supplement the rustic, wood, and wicker furniture already discussed. The primary purpose of a cabin is for owners and guests to relax and be comfortable so the furnishings should be chosen to accomplish this mission.

One of a set of marked oak chairs made by the Stickley Brothers Furniture Co. of Grand Rapids, Michigan, 1915-1920, is pictured with a large round oak table. The branded mark reads "Stickley Bros. Co./Grand Rapids." Arts and Crafts furniture and accessories fit nicely with cabin décor. *Private collection.* (Chairs, $250 each; table $350-$400).

Oak "settle" by Charles P. Limbert & Co. located in Grand Rapids, Michigan, circa 1915. The branded mark reads "Limberts Arts & Crafts Furniture." The figure of a man planing a table is also part of the trademark. The settle has been recovered with cowhide. Pictured with the furniture is a handmade oak floor lamp with an oak and green slag glass shade. An additional cowhide decorates the wall. Private collection. (Settle, not enough examples to determine price).

Left:
A Morris chair with an oak frame works nicely combined with mission or rustic furniture when furnishing a cabin. The chair features a footrest which can be pulled out for use or pushed under the chair for regular seating. The back is also adjustable. The chair is marked "ROYAL EASY CHAIR CO./STURGIS, MICH/ U.S.A./Royal Easy Chairs/Push the Button-Back Reclines." The new upholstery features horses and cowboys. ($200+).

Antique oak stacked bookcase featuring five shelves filled with appropriate cabin collectibles. The glass fronts have been raised so the items inside can be more easily seen. Included are vintage books, postcards, fishing creel, pyrographic items, radio, German bisque Indian doll, canoe, teepee, leather photo albums, oak boxes and a pine tree thermometer. (Bookcase, $600+).

Advertisement for "Royal Easy Chairs" in the 1924 Montgomery Ward catalog which shows chairs similar to the example pictured. The oak chair originally sold for $21.98.

Oversized wicker rocker in the mission style, circa 1920s. It still retains the label which reads "KARPEN Furniture Co./Chicago." The example is very desirable because it still retains its original paint. The seat and back have been recovered. Also shown is a vintage wicker plant stand. It has been repainted. As pictured in the interiors of the early Adirondack camps, wicker blends nicely with both rustic and mission oak furniture in cabins of any age. (Rocker, $325-$350; plant stand, $150).

Advertisement in the Sears Fall and Winter catalog from 1931-1932 which pictures a whole page of fiber-wicker furniture. The furniture could be purchased by the piece or in sets. The most expensive set was priced at $56.50 and included a couch, rocker, straight chair, table, and planter.

This large circa 1920s wicker table has been repainted as have most of the early wicker pieces. Pinecone decorated pottery (See *Pinecone Decorated Pottery, Dinner, and Glassware chapter*) and an art deco brass lamp decorated with the figure of a deer are displayed on the table. The top is made of oak. A wicker straight chair can be seen behind the table. The upholstered chair, circa 1920s, has been recovered in a cowboy fabric. From a vacation home in Arkansas. (Table, $300-$325; lamp, $100; chair, $50).

The Western Look

The western look can be achieved with a mixture of both new and old furniture and accessories as shown in this living room. A vintage highback ranch saddle circa 1930s, saddle bags from the U.S. government, cowboy hats, and a bear skin rug blend nicely with newer furniture pieces and lamps. (Ranch saddle, $300-$400; saddle bags, $150; bear rug, $500-$600.) *From the collection of Jim Shivers.*

Many cabin owners and designers prefer the western look because of its casual appearance. This type of decorating was prevalent in the western states from the early 1900s until the late 1950s. Many lodges, dude ranches, hotels, and private ranches were decorated in this style for decades. Most of the early furnishings were a combination of rustic and western.

It wasn't until Thomas C. Molesworth began making his distinctive furniture that the style was elevated to an art form. Molesworth was born in 1890 and founded his Shoshone Furniture Company in Cody, Wyoming, in 1931. There, he began making ranch furniture using woods, leather, antlers, silhouettes, In-

dian weavings, fringe, tacks, and bright colors. His pieces were decorated with cowboys, Indians, horses, and other wildlife.

The new furniture attracted attention and Molesworth began receiving commissions to provide furnishings for hotels, dude ranches, and rustic retreats. Sometimes he and his wife LaVerne worked together to create the décor for an entire room, according to Molesworth's grandson, Leslie Molesworth-Callahan, who has documented their work. LaVerne was the one who made the drapes and bedspreads. A completed room often included the furniture, lamps, chandelier, rugs, and accessories. Indian or cowboy artifacts were sometimes featured in the décor as well.

By 1960, the western look had fallen out of favor with Molesworth's high end clientele and he closed his business in 1961. Interest in Molesworth was revived in 1989, when an exhibition of his work was held at the Buffalo Bill Historical Center in Cody, Wyoming, and continued in 1990 when his work was shown at the Gene Autry Western Heritage Museum in Los Angeles, California. The artist produced approximately 5,000 to 6,000 pieces during his lifetime, according to Terry Winchell, a Molesworth authority. The golden age of his work was from the mid 1930s until World War II. Molesworth died in 1977.

With the new interest in Molesworth, collectors in the 1990s began searching for examples of his work and prices escalated accordingly. Currently, many new craftsmen are producing similar if not duplicates of Molesworth's designs. For collectors who are fortunate enough to own an original Molesworth piece, this legacy will continue to give them pleasure.

During the 1950s, mainstream America was just beginning to tune into the western look. Perhaps this was due to the many popular western television shows then capturing America's attention, including "Bat Masterson," "Bonanza," "Cheyenne," "Maverick," "Gunsmoke," "Have Gun, Will Travel, "The Life and Legend of Wyatt Earp," and, for the youngsters, shows starring Hopalong Cassidy, Roy Rogers, and Gene Autry. With so much focus on the West, new products were manufactured to take advantage of this ready-made market. Sears and Montgomery Ward catalogs offered rooms of furniture with a western design as well as accessories that included lamps, light fixtures, dinnerware, blankets, and bedspreads. Clothing was also being featured to reflect the continued interest in the western look. Included were men's ties decorated with horses, matching his and hers western shirts, and children's clothing of all types. In addition, children's toys reflected the nation's infatuation with the old West. Many products endorsed by the popular television stars were sold. Children were especially interested in Roy Rogers and Hopalong Cassidy merchandise.

Any of these 1950s and 1960s products can be used in decorating a current cabin to give it a western theme. Commercial items include bedspreads, blankets, and dinnerware, which can still be used for their original purposes. The original Wallace Rodeo dishes signed by artist Till Goodan are also very collectible. They bear the stamp "Westward Ho," and are so expensive that collectors may prefer to purchase the newer reproductions. The originals were produced from the 1940s to the early 1960s. The reproduction pieces do not include Till Goodan's signature.

The toys from the era can be displayed singly or in groups. For a guest bedroom or a bunkroom, several wall shelves filled with western games, lunch boxes, play sets, and other western TV related toys would add a unique touch to the guest quarters. Hanging toys from the era, including guitars, telephones, cowboy hats, chaps, guns, and holsters, could be used on a wall to decorate an entryway or mud room.

A shelf featuring vintage western boots and hats would provide an interesting display area in an entryway. Unique western clothing, along with hand-tooled leather purses and belts, could be arranged on hooks or pegs under the shelf to add additional color to the area.

Besides toys, collections of vintage horse figures could be displayed anywhere in a western cabin. The plastic Breyer horses are particularly popular among collectors because they have been made for so many years in many different models. For those collectors who want something a little unusual, the circa 1950 pot metal horses, made in a variety of sizes, offer an alternative horse collectible. Both types of horses can be displayed on shelves, the tops of bookcases, or on tables in a western themed cabin.

In addition to the commercially made products produced to take advantage of the western craze, authentic ranch and horse related items should also always be included in a cabin decorated with the western look. Vintage saddles can be placed on saddle stands or draped over a cabin banister to add a touch from a working ranch. Old bridles, spurs, chaps, rosettes, and stirrups can be displayed on pegs, on a shelf, or under glass to add reminders of early ranch life.

When using a western theme for decorating, the cabin owner can combine both new and old items to make a comfortable and appealing setting. Currently, new mass produced furniture as well as individual craftsman pieces are being made with western designs. Combined with old accents, accessories, and perhaps some family related items, an interesting and livable cabin retreat or home will emerge.

Leather "wing chair" made by Thomas Molesworth for the Buffalo Bill Village in 1938. Moose antlers were used for the "wings." Big brass tacks decorate the chair. This example is one of only three that are known to exist. Similar chairs are now being produced by contemporary craftsmen. ($60,000-$80,000). *Courtesy of Fighting Bear Antiques.*

The most sought after and expensive western furniture was made by Thomas Molesworth *(see text)*. Pictured is a two-sided writing desk, circa 1938. The desk was intended for use in a hotel or dude ranch. It is thought that less than six examples of this desk were made by the master craftsman. Deer and elk designs decorate the table. A matching keyhole chair accompanies the desk. The back of the chair features a moose silhouette. The top of the table and the seat of the chair were made of leather. The chair was crafted for the Buffalo Village in Cody, Wyoming, in 1938. (Desk, $40,000; chair, $5,000). *Courtesy of Fighting Bear Antiques, Jackson, Wyoming.*

① 134.95 ② 79.95 ③ 27.95 ④ 13.95 ⑥ 19.95 ⑦ 16.95 Each

⑤ 29.95

A full set of similar furniture was advertised in the Montgomery Ward Fall and Winter catalog in 1959. Furniture pieces included a sofa bed, platform rocker and foot stool, two end tables, coffee table, occasional chair, and cowboy boot lamps. The set sold for $269.95, not including the chair or one of the lamps.

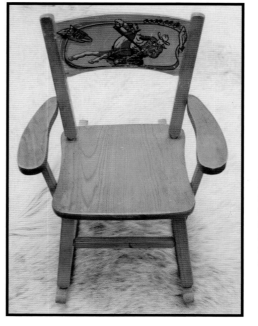

Although most collectors can't afford to decorate a cabin with the expensive Thomas Molesworth pieces, mass produced "western" furniture from the 1950s is still available. The back of this chair features a horse's head and a wood wagon wheel design is under the arms. A cowhide hangs in the background. (Chair, $225; cowhide, $250+). *From the collection of Jim Shivers.*

Many different children's rocking chairs were sold in the 1950s which featured western designs. This one does not tie-in to a specific cowboy hero like some of the chairs of the era, including one which represented Hopalong Cassidy. ($85). *Courtesy of Deborah Taylor of Taylor and Taylor Design.*

The older lamps from the 1950s with a western look are especially appealing to collectors. Pictured is a lamp with a wood stirrup base and its original western shade. This type of lamp was sometimes designed for a boy's bedroom. ($100+). *Lamp from the collection of Jim Shivers.*

This vintage metal and glass light fixture is circa 1950s. Western brands have been cut out of the metal so the light shines through the openings. The fixture is 13" in diameter and the metal sides are 5" tall. ($50). *Photograph and fixture from the Shivers collection.*

This is one of two western lamps originally purchased in the 1950s and both still remain in the family. The lamp base is shaped like a saddle on a fence. The decoration on the shade features cactus and a fence with mountains in the background. ($200-$300 for the pair). *Shivers collection.*

Metal light fixture apparently produced by the same unknown company, circa 1950s. An identical "spur" decoration hangs from the bottom of the fixture. Four hurricane shades cover the light bulbs. ($75+). *Photograph and fixture from the Shivers collection.*

73

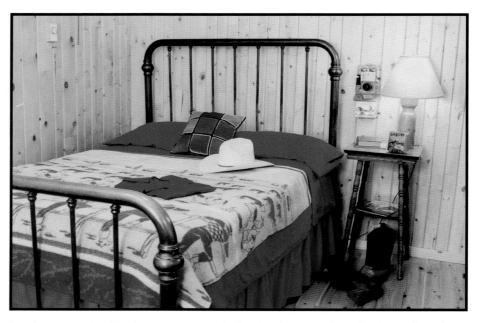

This wagon wheel light fixture is one of several which remain in use at Betty's Café and Bakery near Grand Lake, Colorado. The light fixtures are original to the restaurant building, which was constructed in 1946. At one time, a restaurant called the Rustic Lantern occupied the building. Similar vintage light fixtures would be perfect to use in a cabin great room decorated with a western theme. (Not enough examples to determine a price.) *Courtesy of Betty's Café & Bakery at Grand River Inn.*

Another example of a vintage western blanket has been used as a bedspread on this cabin bed, along with a red comfort, sheets, and pillow cases. A western hat, shirt, and boots are also pictured. A toy ranch phone hangs on the wall and vintage western books decorate the small table. (Blanket, $85+).

Other practical western decorative items that can be used in cabins of today are the light-weight blankets made during earlier years. This advertisement for Lone Ranger blankets appeared in the Montgomery Ward Fall and Winter catalog in 1955-1956. The ad copy stated that the blankets were the "official Lone Ranger" blankets. The Lone Ranger was a popular radio, television, and movie personality during the 1940s and 1950s. The blankets were made of 90% rayon and 10% nylon and sold for $3.39 each.

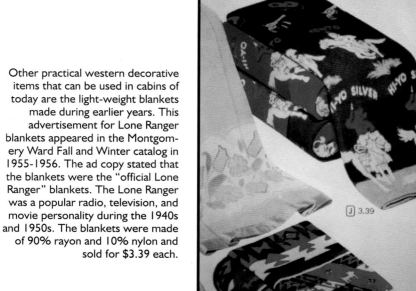

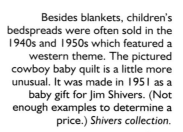

Besides blankets, children's bedspreads were often sold in the 1940s and 1950s which featured a western theme. The pictured cowboy baby quilt is a little more unusual. It was made in 1951 as a baby gift for Jim Shivers. (Not enough examples to determine a price.) *Shivers collection.*

Monterrey Western Ware plate, bowl, and cup. The pieces are marked "Monterrey Western Ware/Made in Mexico." (Bowl, $20-$25). *Shivers collection.*

Vintage dishes, decorated with western designs, also offer an interesting cabin collectible. These items can be used for display or for dinnerware. The metal Monterrey Western Ware line is especially popular for collectors. Pictured are several pieces of the Western Ware displayed in a vintage oak rack. (Plates, $20-$25 each; cups, $15-$20 each; cream and sugar set, $140; platter, $90-$100). *Shivers collection.*

Western Ware cream and sugar showing the design used on several of the pieces. *Shivers collection.*

Sauce pot and coffee pot from the Monterrey Western Ware line. In addition, a skillet, serving tray, and vegetable bowl were made in this design. (Sauce pot, $150; coffee pot, $125-$175). *Shivers collection.*

In addition to the yellow metal dishes, an unmarked brown and white set was also produced. This metal line featured a steer head for decoration. These examples are harder to find. Shown is the coffee pot from the series ($150+). *Shivers collection.*

Cups and plates were also produced in the line. (Plate, $20-$25; cup, $15-$20). *Shivers collection.*

Another interesting brand of western-related dinnerware is the Wallace Rodeo pattern, which is being reproduced due to its popularity. Pictured is a plate, circa 1940s to early 1960s, marked with the artist's signature, "Till Goodan." The back of the plate is marked "Westward Ho/Rodeo Pattern/made in California U.S.A./Wallace China." The current pieces do not include the artist's signature. (Original plate, $100+).

This contemporary dining room is decorated with a 1950s western lamp, vintage metal tableware, and family horse related photographs to add to the western look. *Shivers collection.*

Four glass mugs with leather holders circa 1970s. Besides mugs, several sizes of glasses were also produced with leather sleeves. *($20 each). Shivers collection.*

Children have enjoyed dressing up like cowboys since the early part of the 20th century. *The Youth's Companion* for Oct. 21, 1909 advertised a cowboy suit and lariat from size 6-14. The outfit was priced at $1.85. The hat was made of straw and the pants were made of khaki cloth and were decorated with fringe down the sides. No outfits were provided for girls. Sears Christmas catalog for 1940 offered a full page of cowboy costumes including one designed for little girls (times change). The prices ranged from 97¢ to $2.89. Any vintage children's western clothing can add an interesting decorating touch to a cabin room.

In addition to the more recent products, prints, plates, calendars, bookends, pyrography items (*See Early Pyrography Pieces chapter),* and other older merchandise was produced which featured the horse's image. Most of these items would also be suitable for use in decorating a modern cabin. Pictured is a 1911 calendar plate advertising Saenger Bros., a hardware store in Sylvan Grove, Kansas. The back is marked "Colonial Co." ($35-$45). *Shivers collection.*

This Annie Oakley cowgirl outfit was manufactured by Leslie-Henry Company, Inc., Mount Vernon, New York, circa 1955. The clothing and box could be displayed on a shelf, along with other western children's clothing or combined with other Annie Oakley items made at the time of the Oakley television show during the 1950s. Paper doll books, coloring books, children's records, games, a lunch box, and reading books were all produced bearing the Annie Oakley name. ($75-$100).

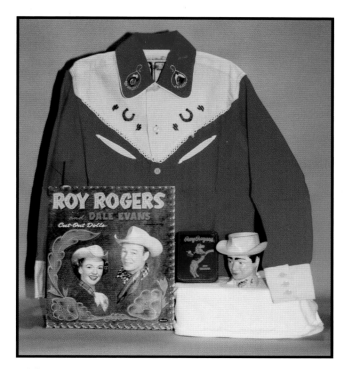

Roy Rogers and Gene Autry children's clothing was also marketed during the 1950s. Pictured is a Roy Rogers shirt which includes the label "Roy Rogers Frontier Shirts, created by Rob Roy, size 12." ($50-$75). Also shown is a "Roy Rogers and Dale Evans Cut-out Dolls" book, No. 1950 (Whitman Publishing Co.) copyright 1954 by Frontiers, Inc., ($85+), Roy Rogers and Trigger 1950s billfold ($40-$50) and a Roy Rogers plastic souvenir cup from Quaker Oats, also from the 1950s ($18-$22). Any of these items can be used with other collectibles to give a touch of nostalgia to a cabin.

Children's or adult's western clothing can also be displayed on pegs. A child's room, bunkroom, or entry hall could provide wall space for such an arrangement. Pictured is a circa 1950s wood rack decorated with the faces of both a girl and a boy and labeled "Hats and Guns." A vintage child's straw cowboy hat and a pair of little boy's chaps have been hung on the pegs. (Rack, $30; chaps, $20; and cowboy hat, $20).

Vintage play sets picturing western scenes can also be used to give a nostalgic touch to a cabin using a western decorating theme. A set could be displayed on a shelf or on a table top to allow more pieces to be seen. This one is the "Roy Rogers Ranch Set" made by Louis Marx and Co., circa early to mid 1950s. The boxed set includes a metal bunkhouse, cowboys, animals, fence, and furniture. ($175+).

Additional Roy Rogers related collectibles include this toy guitar that could be hung on a cabin wall. This fiberboard example was made by Jefferson in the 1950s. ($55-$75). A "Roy Rogers Picture Frame Tray Inlay Puzzle" No. 4426 is also shown. It was made by Whitman Publishing Co. and was copyrighted by Frontiers, Inc. in 1958 ($25-$35). A group of western-related puzzles could be framed to make another interesting wall arrangement to carry out a western theme.

Another of the "big three" famous children's television heroes of the 1950s was Gene Autry. This grouping includes a 17" Gene Autry plastic doll made by Terri Lee, Inc., in 1949. He is wearing his original shirt and pants marked "Gene Autry," ($600+). Other Gene Autry related material includes a record album called "Gene Autry's Western Classics" from 1947 issued by the Columbia Recording Corp., ($35), a lobby card from the Autry film *Riders in the Sky* from Columbia Pictures Corp., dated 1949 ($35) and "Red River Valley" sheet music from the 1936 Republic film of the same name published by Calumet Music Co. in Chicago ($15). Two Gene Autry books are also pictured. They include a Better Little Book called *Gene Autry Cowboy Detective* published by Whitman Publishing Co. in 1940 ($30+) and *Gene Autry and the Redwood Pirates* also from Whitman Publishing in 1946 ($10-$15).

A shelf of western related children's lunch boxes would also add color to a cabin or log home. Lunch boxes were produced to promote Roy Rogers, Hopalong Cassidy, and Gene Autry, plus the TV programs "Bonanza," "Gunsmoke," "Have Gun, Will Travel," and "Wagon Train," as well as several others. Pictured is a "Bonanza" lunch box marketed by Aladdin Industries, circa 1965. It carries a copyright from the National Broadcasting Co. ($75+). Instead of lunch boxes, western related coloring books could be displayed in discarded church hymnal racks to provide a similar splash of cabin color. The "Bonanza" coloring book shown dates from the 1960s and was published by the Salfield Publishing Co.

Western toys that can be hung on the wall could contribute to interesting groupings. This lithographed metal Ranch Phone is a replacement for one of the co-author's valued childhood toys. The circa 1950s phone is marked "A Gong Bell Toy/The Gong Bell Mfg. Co./East Hampton, Conn./Made in the U.S.A." Pictured with the phone is a *Cowboys in Pop-up Action Pictures* book by E. Joseph Dreany, published by Maxton Publishers, Inc., New York, 1951. (Phone, $65+; book, $15-$20).

The third member of the top three television cowboy stars of the 1950s was Hopalong Cassidy played by William Boyd. Collectibles from this star can also add interest to a western cabin. Pictured is a Hopalong Cassidy doll made by Ideal in 1949. He is missing his hat. The 18" doll has a vinyl head and a stuffed body. ($350). Also shown is a *Hopalong Cassidy Coloring Book Starring William Boyd* (No. 1200). It was copyrighted in 1950 by Doubleday and Co. and published by Samuel Lowe Co. ($40+).

Related family toys are always fun to use in decorating, especially in a cabin. Pictured is a No. 6300 Nylint horse van, circa early to mid 1960s. The metal truck-van came with two plastic horses which fit through the opening doors of the trailer. This was a favorite toy of the co-author. It measures 23" long. Shown above the van are two horse-related family photographs picturing two of the family's horses from long ago. (Truck, $100+).

The western look can be found in many different products. Pictured is a tie rack decorated with a horse's head as well as two neckties which also feature horse's heads. All three items are circa 1950. The tie rack was produced of a composition-type material made to look like wood. Both ties are labeled "Hand Painted." Sears Christmas catalog for 1950 offered similar ties decorated with horse's heads, birds, and dog heads for 97¢ each. Those ties were made of rayon crepe. (Tie rack, $15; ties, $12-$15 each).

Although many different designs of horse-related bookends have been designed over the years, this metal bookrack made with real horse shoes is unique. It holds an assortment of books on western subjects, including *The First Book of Horses* by McLennan McMeekin, published by Franklin Watts, New York, 1949, a Gene Autry adventure, and two old novels by B.M. Bower from the 1920s and 1930s. They include *Chip of the Flying-U* and *Flying-U-Ranch,* both Grosset and Dunlap Publications. (Bookrack, $8-$10; books, $10-$15 each).

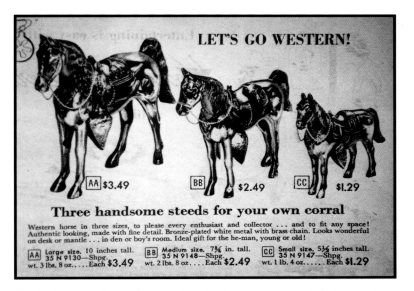

Breyer plastic horses have become very collectible in recent years and several books have been written about the different models that have been produced. A collection could be displayed on a shelf or on a table top to add interest to a cabin room. These two examples of Breyer paint horses are circa 1970s. ($55-$60 each). *From the Jim Shivers collection.*

In addition to the Breyer horses, there has been a recent revival of interest in the pot metal horses of the late 1940s and 1950s. These horses were advertised in the Sears Christmas catalog of 1950 in three different sizes. Included were 5.5" ($1.29), 7.75" ($2.49), and 10" ($3.49). The description states that the horses were made of "Bronze-plated white metal with brass chain." The text recommended that they be displayed in a den or boy's room, on a mantel or a desk.

A small collection of hand-tooled leather goods can also add a different look when displayed in a western cabin. Purses, belts, billfolds, key holders, satchels, and other items have been made of tooled leather for decades. Workmanship and prices vary from one example to another so prices are hard to determine. Pictured are a dark-colored purse circa 1950s and a light-colored purse and belt of more recent vintage (1950s purse, $35+; newer purse $20-$25; belt, $8).

A collection of horses like those shown in the Sears catalog in 1950 is pictured on a table top. Five different sizes of the horses are represented from 2.75" to 10" tall. Included are two of the co-author's childhood horses that were used to begin the collection. Their permanent home is the top of an oak stacked bookcase. ($12-$25 each).

This vintage leather snapshot album could share a table top with a small collection of the metal horses. For a family with a horse connection, old photographs picturing horses and family members could be mounted inside. The outside of the old album is decorated with a cowboy on a bucking horse. This item, which has never been used, was a souvenir from Boulder, Colorado. ($20).

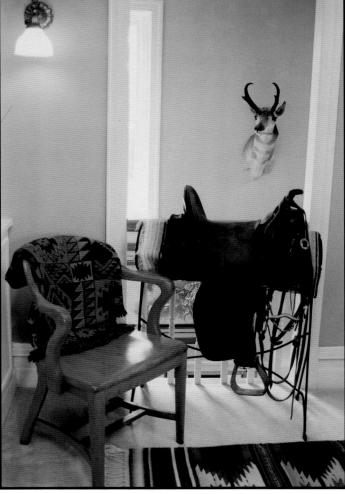

Saddles can be displayed on stands or placed over a stair railing in a cabin setting. This old ranch saddle, complete with wood stirrups and bit rests on a stand. An antelope trophy is on the wall in the background. An old oak office chair, vintage wall light fixture, a blanket, and a rug complete the setting. (Saddle, $200+). *Shivers collection.*

In addition to western related collectibles of the various types already shown, some space needs to be left to display authentic items used on the ranch. The most important of these examples is the saddle. Those that have some connection to the cabin's owner are especially appealing. Pictured is a "Billy Cook" roper saddle, circa 1950s. The current owner used it when showing horses some thirty years ago. The saddle is now displayed on a stand in front of a cowhide wall hanging. ($1,500-$2,000). *From the collection of Jim Shivers.*

In addition to saddles, other cowboy and horse related memorabilia can also add to a cabin's décor. Pictured is an original Argentine Brow Bard bridle and Snaffle bit, circa late 1920s. The bit includes a silver inlay shank. Also shown is a pair of leather chaps with buck stitching, circa 1970s. The items hang from a handmade bridle holder. (Bridle and bit, $2,500; chaps, $300). *Shivers collection.*

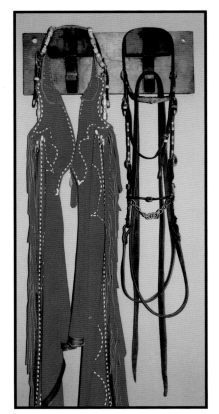

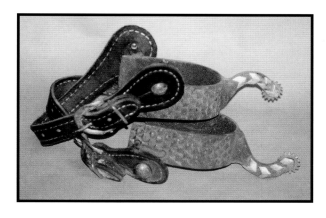

Smaller horse-related items can be displayed on shelves or under glass. These interesting spurs date from the 1940s or 1950s. They are decorated with sliver inlay. ($150-$175 pair). *Shivers collection.*

Below:
Wood stirrups are also collectible. They can be used as towel holders, part of a lamp base or displayed along with a collection of spurs and rosettes. ($45-$50 pair). *Shivers collection.*

Other western related items include mounted horns or skulls from bulls. The pictured example probably comes from a Jersey Bull. The items are more valuable if the horns are still intact and have the horn caps in place. This one is missing the outside covering of the horns. The skulls can be hung on a cabin wall or used for an exterior accent. ($65). *Shivers collection.*

The Indian Connection

Many of the firms who produced pyrographic items for hobbyists featured Indian pictures on several of their products. Shown are two tie racks, both decorated with Indian chief designs. The bottom tie rack was sold by the Flemish Art Company during the early 1900s. The tie rack on the top is a much later product, probably dating from the 1930s. Unlike the Flemish items which were to be burnt by the hobbyist, this later design was sold as a completed souvenir from Phoenix, Arizona. (Indian and canoe, $30-$40, souvenir, $15+).

Cabins have been decorated using Indian made rugs, baskets, pottery, and other hand-made Native American items since the early 1900s. Today, similar museum-like treasures are being used to decorate some of the most exclusive vacation properties in the Western and Southwestern regions of the country. Many books have been written describing and pricing these Indian artifacts, which has resulted in new and continued interest by collectors and decorators.

Although these high-end Indian items remain popular as investments and decorating accents, the surprising trend of today is the interest being shown in the less-expensive items that were purchased by tourists as souvenirs. While some of these products were hand-made by Indian tribes, many other companies took advantage of the Indian mystique and marketed commercially-produced souvenirs by adding an Indian image or decal to the item.

Collectors are now buying vintage souvenir birch canoes, wood paddles, pipes and pennants to add to their homes. Some of these items are decorated with an Indian decal while the older pennants are printed with Indian and canoe scenes.

Leather and suede Indian decorated souvenir items are also popular. They include tie racks, photo albums, and address and autograph books. (See Paper Collectibles chapter for more examples.)

The Indian dolls, sold as souvenirs through many decades, are especially desirable. The most popular are those referred to as "Skookum" models. The dolls came in sizes ranging from 6" to 36" tall. Collectors prefer to purchase these dolls in all original condition. Since most were never intended to be played with, many of the dolls are still found in surprisingly good shape. The dolls were produced in the images of men, women, and children, and sometimes the women dolls included a papoose.

Besides souvenirs, there is a new interest in old calendars and pictures which featured Indian subjects. There is so much demand that many of the early calendars and prints are being reproduced.

Even old sheet music, which includes Indian-related covers have become popular. Surprisingly, quite a number of these sheets were published in the early 1900s.

With the interest in anything "Indian," old children's books and bookends have also gained popularity. Some of these early books featuring Indians blend nicely with the old birch bark canoes and teepee souvenirs. If space is available, a vintage canoe can be hung from the ceiling or a collection of authentic paddles can be mounted on a wall.

Because of the interest in the Indian image during the early part of the twentieth century, many of the products sold by the Flemish Art Company and other wood-burning pyrographic firms featured Indian motifs. Although these companies produced hundreds of designs, the Indian-related products have become especially collectible. (See also Early Pyrography Pieces chapter.) Any of these items can be combined to use in the decoration of a cabin. Using a wall, shelves, or a tabletop, these Indian souvenirs can add color and interest to an old or new cabin.

Birch bark canoes were made to be used for pincushions as well as souvenirs. This "Canoe Pincushion" was advertised in the Sears Fall and Winter catalog for 1931-1932. It was 5.5" in length and sold for 15¢.

Souvenir wood items featuring Indian decal decorations. The pipe measures 10" long and the paddle is 19". These paddles are especially collectible. (Pipe, $20+; paddle, $75-$90).

Early souvenir felt pennants were sometimes entirely decorated with a picture. The ones featuring Indian scenes are especially collectible. Both of these pennants show Indian maidens paddling canoes. They are approximately 21" long. These pennants are from Bangor, Maine and Watkins Glen, New York. ($25-$30 each).

This leather postcard and small Indian-decorated handkerchief offer two more souvenir products with the popular Indian theme. The printing on the front of the postcard reads "INDIAN CHIEF/the OLDEST INHABITANT." The other side of the postcard is stamped "POST CARD" with a place for a stamp. An address would have been hard to read if it had been written on the leather. This card was never sent through the mail. The handkerchief is made of rayon and is marked "CANADA." (Postcard, $6-$10; hankie, $10).

Leather address book sold as a souvenir from Lake George, New York. An Indian brave is pictured on the cover. A Lake George "linen" postcard mailed in 1936 is also shown. (Address book, $10+; postcard, $5-$8).

Felt pennants circa 1940s and 1950s still featured Indian scenes, but the printed pictures were much smaller and male figures were used to paddle the canoes instead of the earlier use of the Indian maiden. Pennants are from Green Mountains, Vermont and LaCrosse, Wisconsin. ($15-$30 each).

Small photo album and autograph book both made of leather-suede and decorated with Indian Chief pictures. The autograph book is marked "Greeley, Colo." and the "Chief Big Feather" photo album was a souvenir from Cheyenne, Wyoming. (Autograph book, $25; photo album, $15-$20).

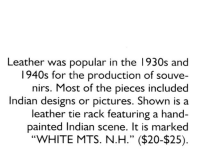

Leather was popular in the 1930s and 1940s for the production of souvenirs. Most of the pieces included Indian designs or pictures. Shown is a leather tie rack featuring a hand-painted Indian scene. It is marked "WHITE MTS. N.H." ($20-$25).

This small suede souvenir needle holder features an Indian Chief as decoration on its front. It is marked "Nelson, B.C." ($3-$5).

Dolls dressed in Indian costumes were made throughout the 20th century and are still being produced. Pictured are four of these dolls, each made from a different type of material. The oldest doll is the 9" tall one on the right. She is circa 1915 to early 1920s and was made in Germany. She is all original and has a brown bisque head, glass eyes, open mouth with teeth, and a 5-piece composition jointed body. Her costume is made of felt. Since her clothes are not removable, the only visible mark is "8/0" on the back of her neck. ($135+). The largest doll was made by the Reliable Toy Company of Toronto, Canada. He is 12.5" tall, made of composition, circa late 1930s to early 1940s. He has painted features, a black mohair wig, and is jointed at the shoulders and hips. Marked on the back of his head is "RELIABLE/MADE IN CANADA." He is wearing his original clothing except for the vintage beaded moccasins that have been added. A 12" "Skookum" doll is also pictured. These types of Indian dolls were sold as souvenirs for decades and are now very much in demand. All of the dolls were made with arms folded beneath a blanket. This doll has wooden legs, paper-type shoes, mohair wig, painted features, and a head made of a composition-type material. The more recent dolls of this type wore plastic shoes. ($125). The fourth doll is a typical Indian souvenir doll like those that have been sold for the last forty years or more. Basic 8" plastic dolls are turned into Indians through the use of paint, wigs, and clothing. ($10).

A collection of Indian Skookum dolls ranging in size from the 4" papoose to the 16" tall Indian male. Each of the larger dolls has a different modeled face. The bigger dolls are much harder to locate and bring higher prices when found in excellent condition. The other two larger dolls are approximately 10" and 12" tall. The 12" doll carries a papoose inside her blanket. The small papoose and seated dolls are 4" tall. The labels sometimes found on the dolls read "Trade Mark Registered/Skookum (Bully Good)/INDIAN Patented." The labels are usually on the doll's foot. (16" doll, $200+; 10"-12" dolls, $100+; dolls with papoose, $150+; seated doll, $50+; papoose, $25+). *Photographs and dolls from the collection of Marilyn Pittman.*

A seated 4" Skookum doll along with her original unmarked mailing box. A cotton ball was used for packing. ($60+). *Pittman collection.*

17" tall leather tepee with beading and leather designs. Although the doll and other accessories are not original to the tepee, they add to the interesting display. (Tepee, $125+). *Pittman collection.*

A collection of vintage cigar or cigarette "silks" featuring Indian designs could make an interesting display. They can be framed or mounted under glass on a coffee table. ($5-$15 each, according to size). *Pittman collection.*

Besides dolls, other toys with an Indian connection have been popular through the years. This advertisement from *The Youth's Companion* from Oct. 21, 1909, pictures a bow and arrow for 75¢, an Indian suit complete with headdress priced at $1.85, and a wigwam for $2.00. It was 6.5' high and 6' in diameter at the base. A cowboy suit and lariat was also available and sold for $1.85.

Besides souvenirs and toys, calendars and prints featuring Indian-related images have also been popular over the years. The December 1918 *Farmer's Wife* magazine pictured a 1919 calendar and a 110-piece Christmas set for only 75¢. The Christmas set included an assortment of stickers, tags, tree decorations, and postcards. The calendar was decorated with an Indian maiden paddling a canoe.

In addition to calendars, other prints were produced in the early 1900s through the 1920s which featured Indians as the subject of the pictures. Shown is the popular Indian on horseback print marked the "Columbian Colortype Co. Chicago" circa late 1920s. The print is approximately 12" x 16". It is in its original frame ($35-$40).

Original calendar sample featuring an Indian maiden circa 1920s. It has no advertisement or calendar pad since it was used as a sample. 22" x 14". ($60).

Small print called "Princess of the Blue Ridge" by E.R. Harder circa late 1920s. It has been re-framed. Postcards from the early part of the century also sometimes featured "Indian Maidens." Pictured are two from the era which have been newly framed. (Re-framed print, $25+; framed postcards, $25-$30 each).

A more recent picture is this "Paint by Number" Indian Maiden circa 1950s to 1960s. There were several different companies who produced a variety of different pictures to be painted by the customer. The painter followed the pre-printed numbers and lines on the picture and was rewarded, if skilled enough, by a "masterpiece" like this one. There are quite a number of collectors buying the "paint by number" pictures and the 50th anniversary of the inventive process was recently celebrated with a museum showing in New York City. (Unframed picture, $10-$15; framed and matted, $20-$25).

Woman's magazines from the 1920s sometimes included a print that was made of heavy paper and ready to be framed. This one came from *Pictorial Review* in 1927. It is called "In a Bad Fix," by W.R. Leigh and was copyrighted by *Pictorial Review* in 1927 courtesy of Babcock Galleries, New York. Print is 14" wide x 11" high. (Unframed, $8-$10).

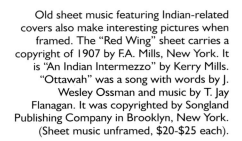

Old sheet music featuring Indian-related covers also make interesting pictures when framed. The "Red Wing" sheet carries a copyright of 1907 by F.A. Mills, New York. It is "An Indian Intermezzo" by Kerry Mills. "Ottawah" was a song with words by J. Wesley Ossman and music by T. Jay Flanagan. It was copyrighted by Songland Publishing Company in Brooklyn, New York. (Sheet music unframed, $20-$25 each).

Pyrographic wood glove box decorated with the head of an Indian chief and other Indian designs. The back of the box is marked "March 13, 1911/ GMB." The inside is lined and padded. ($50+).

The Pioneers, circa 1915 by J. Fenimore Cooper features an Indian on the cover. This edition was published by Grosset & Dunlap in New York. It is supported with bookends circa 1940 to 1950s which feature an Indian brave on horseback shooting a rifle. The bookends are made of a composition type material to give them the look of wood. (Book, $20; bookends, $25).

Large pyrographic picture featuring an Indian maiden and other Indian décor. It may be that it was to hold a calendar in the lighter square at the bottom, but the hobbyist who completed the project decorated this part as well. 21" high x 9.75" wide. ($50+).

A collection of Indian-related souvenirs decorates the top of this small oak chest. Included are birch bark canoes, tepee, drum, and basket, along with two pairs of moccasins and a papoose Indian doll. The tiny canoe and Indian doll are "mailers." Tags were attached to small items with space for an address and a stamp so the souvenir could be dropped into a mailbox and sent to a friend or relative. The canoe was mailed with a 1 1/2 cent stamp. The back of the tag reads, "I am sending this little birch canoe, filled with good wishes and greetings, to you. From Raton, New Mex." (Largest canoe, $20-$25).

A collection of tie racks and other Indian decorated pieces that could be used to decorate a wall. Tie racks not already described include one featuring an Indian Chief decal on a piece of wood with bark still showing ($45), an Indian birch bark canoe rack ($20-$25), and another style of pyrographic rack ($25-$30).

Old wood ironing boards make interesting display tables. They can be used in a variety of heights with the wood exposed or with an added camp blanket to give color to the display. Indian dolls, books, and a vintage toy headdress are in this arrangement. The books include *Eagle Eye: Our Little Indian Friend and Other Captivating Stories for Boys and Girls* by Mrs. Belle Manley Stayton, copyright 1901 by L.G. Stahl, ($20-$25), *Shining Star the Indian Boy* by Hattie A. Walker, copyright 1932 by Beckley-Cardy Co., ($10-$12), *Winona A Little Indian of the Prairies*, copyright 1935 by Platt & Munk Co. ($10-$12), and *My Indian Book* by Bruce Grant, copyright 1958 by Rand McNally & Co., ($8). The vintage headdress has an old felt headband decorated with printed Indian pictures circa 1940s, ($20-$25). The ironing board is covered with an old camp blanket featuring Indian designs.

A whole room of both new and old Indian collectibles is shown. Included are dolls, books, pictures, toys, camp blankets, lamps, plates, statues, wind chimes, rugs, drums, and much more. Just a small amount of the collection is pictured here. *Photographs and Indian items from the collection of Marge Meisinger.*

Early Pyrography Pieces

During the early 1900s, the hobby of pyrography (wood-burning) became popular with both men and women. The burning could be done on plush, wood, or leather, although wood was the most popular medium. Once stored away in attics or otherwise discarded, many of these items are turning up in flea markets or antique shops and are being used as rustic accents in today's cabins.

In its heyday, many companies carried the necessary materials for hobbyists interested in learning the craft of pyrography. The most prolific was the Flemish Art Company in Brooklyn, New York. The firm's early catalogs offered an interesting array of wood products that could be finished using the company's offerings. The cheapest pyrography outfits included only the basics (instruction booklet, alcohol lamp, double rubber bulb, Benzine bottle, cork handle, and point) contained in a pyrographic box. The package sold for $1.70. More expensive sets were also available. The most expensive ensemble sold for $8.50. It included more of each item plus stain, watercolors, brushes, a carving set, and a fancier container.

The Flemish firm used different designs on its products and most items were made in each of the popular patterns. Merchandise featuring Gibson-type ladies and Indian décor were best sellers. The customer purchased the item with the design already on the object and using the pyrographic (wood-burning) technique, followed the lines of the design to complete the project. Although some hobbyists painted the picture once it was finished, today's cabin owners usually prefer the items with no color added.

The Flemish offerings included various sizes of plaques and pictures, a variety of picture frames to hold one, two, three, or four photographs, and boxes of all sizes, which were made for many different purposes. The smallest boxes were to hold stamps and the largest were to be used for shirtwaists. These large boxes measured 15.5" x 16.25" x 27". In between these sizes were boxes produced to hold jewelry, postcards, handkerchiefs, gloves, collars and cuffs, photos, cards, poker chips, neckties, and boxes of several sizes to be used on dressers. Zinc-lined humidor boxes were also available.

More unusual pyrography items produced by the Flemish Art Company included a large offering of tie racks, towel racks, pipe racks, ashtrays, smoking sets, match scratchers and holders, key racks, souvenir spoon holders, paper cutters, nut bowls, call bells, pin trays, hand mirrors, brushes, nut pick sets, comb, tray and brush, thermometers, whisk broom holders, broom holders, stationary racks, calendars, and clock stands.

Larger pyrography products included many sizes and designs of waste baskets, steins, book racks, checker boards, plate racks, trays, shaving mirrors and shaving cup racks, comb and brush racks, small tables or plant stands, jardinière stands, and foot stools.

A small offering of furniture pieces was also included in the Flemish catalogs. Included were a folding round table, parlor table, piano bench, umbrella stand, wall mirror, combination piano stool and music rack, combination chair and table, hall chair, arm chair, bookcase, and writing desk. The most expensive item was the bookcase for $10. Most of the boxes, plaques, and other small items were priced from 25¢ to $1.00 each.

Pyrographic designs most appealing to cabin decorators are those which feature Indian maidens, chiefs, canoes, deer or other wildlife, acorns, horses, and the specialty series picturing women participating in various sports. If a collector wants to display a variety of pyrography products, other designs could be used as well.

Besides the Flemish Art Company, other firms offered a variety of pyrography products. Thayer and Chandler was advertising its products in the early 1900s in *The Cosmopolitan* magazine. This firm sold items, which carried designs done on plush, wood, or leather. Their catalog totaled seventy-two pages with twenty-four pages in color. A total of 1,000 items were featured in the catalog.

The Montgomery Ward catalog circa 1916 carried two finished "hand burnt" leather pillow slips. One of them featured an Indian chief while the other pictured a deer. Both pillows were decorated with fringe and leather lacing around the edges. They sold for $2.05 each.

The Youth's Companion offered pyrographic materials in 1909. Sets to use in the process of doing pyrography were featured as well as eighteen different products ranging in price from 15¢ to $1.75 each. Leather was also available for those who wanted to use that medium.

The art of pyrography was revived briefly circa 1930s and 1940s when many souvenirs were sold decorated with simple designs. It is not known what company was responsible for the items but they can still be found easily and are very reasonably priced. A wall shelf unit would make a nice way to display these products as they were sometimes made in unusual shapes.

Although the interest in pyrography eventually ended, boys continued to receive "wood burning" sets into the 1950s and early 1960s, usually as Christmas gifts.

For today's collectors, the early pyrography boxes, plaques, picture frames, and other items can add a rustic look and a touch of nostalgia to a cabin table, shelf, or wall. The larger pieces (umbrella stand, large boxes, furniture) can also be used in cabin décor, but they are much harder to find in good condition. (See *Indian Connection chapter* for more examples of pyrographic items.)

This pyrography frame holds a baby picture of one of the authors sitting in the old basket sharing self space beside it. The basket is at least seventy-five years old. The birch shelf is a new product. These collectibles could be added anywhere in a cabin to add rustic accents. (Frame, $40-$45; basket, $60+).

Pyrography box which was sold as a container to hold items to be used in finishing the box as well as for other projects. ($40-$45 with accessories).

The Youth's Companion for Oct. 21, 1909 featured a different "Pyrography Outfit." The copy reads, "The Pyrography Outfit here offered is our new Expert, which contains the Farney Carburetor and Blast Pipe. This Carburetor gives out a superior gas, cannot tip over, and also displaces the use of a glass lamp and alcohol for heating the points. This necessity is met by the use of an attached Blast Pipe." The price listed was $3.25 for outfit.

Although the products are no longer usable, they include a Benzine bottle, tubing, alcohol lamp, two rubber bulbs with net, cork handle, curved point, and point box. Missing is the instruction booklet. This was a very basic set and likely sold for around $2.00. It appears to be from the Flemish Art Company.

The same Youth's Companion also offered a number of stamped articles for burning. Items included trinket tray, handkerchief box, calendar, photography frame, nut bowl, jewel box, extension book rack, hair receiver, key rack, glove box, match safe, and jardinière stand. They were priced from 15¢ to $1.75 each.

Another Flemish Art Company box which features a popular decoration of three horse's heads. This design was also used on a variety of products. This box was designed to hold handkerchiefs. ($30+). *From the collection of Jim Shivers.*

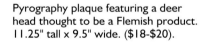

Pyrography plaque featuring a deer head thought to be a Flemish product. 11.25" tall x 9.5" wide. ($18-$20).

Matching pyrography box decorated with the same deer head as pictured on the plaque. Since the Flemish Art Company used the same designs on a variety of items, a small collection could be assembled using only the deer head designs. ($25+).

Indian maiden pyrography plaque, circa 1910. The plaque is marked on the back "FLEMISH/858/ART" along with what appears to be the original price of 15¢.

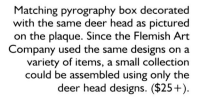

Flemish glove box nicely decorated with acorns. The Flemish boxes also included the same design on the inside cover as appeared on the top of the box. The decoration on this box blends nicely with rustic décor. ($30+).

The series of "Women's Sports" boxes is especially appealing. Probably Flemish products, the boxes featured women circa 1915 participating in sports. The golfer box is a double box which opens from both sides. Old handkerchiefs are still inside. The bathing beauty glove box is equally attractive. Both boxes have been painted. ($50-$60 each).

Other boxes in the "Women's Sports" series include the ice skater and skier. Not pictured is the tennis scene. Although both of these boxes have been painted, the color on the skater box is poorly done which lowers its value. (Skater glove box, $25; skier handkerchief box, $50-$60).

Pyrographic boxes were made in many different sizes. These include a box marked "Post Cards," one titled "Jewels," and a small box that may have been meant for stamps. Postcard boxes can be filled with postcards important to the cabin owner and placed on a table so that visitors and owners alike can enjoy browsing through the collection. (Postcard box, $45+; jewel box, $35; stamp box, $25).

Three picture frames finished with the pyrography process. Many different designs and sizes of frames were produced. The largest frame carried by the Flemish Art Company had spaces for four pictures. Old family photographs have been placed in the frames. (Small, $18-$25; large, $35-$40; two-picture frame, not as nicely finished, $25-$30).

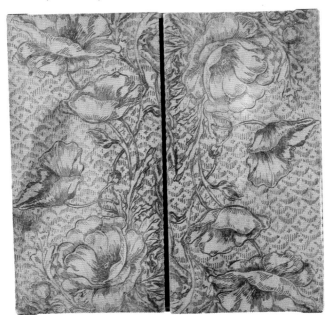

Double boxes are a little more unusual and were likely made to hold handkerchiefs. This one is decorated with a nice flower design. Probably a Flemish product. ($25-$35).

Pyrography book rack. The sides can be pulled out to accommodate more books. Even the bottom of the rack is decorated with flowers. ($40-$50).

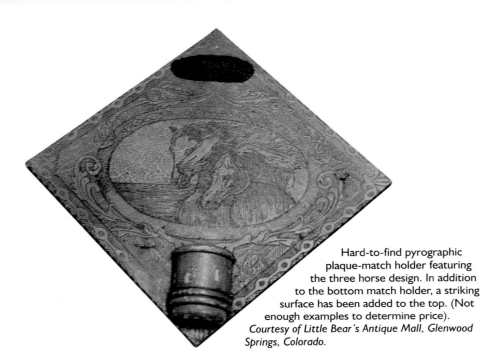

Hard-to-find pyrographic plaque-match holder featuring the three horse design. In addition to the bottom match holder, a striking surface has been added to the top. (Not enough examples to determine price). *Courtesy of Little Bear's Antique Mall, Glenwood Springs, Colorado.*

Utensil or silverware tote that is also an unusual pyrography product. 11.25" long x 7" wide. ($30-$35).

Unusual pyrography spoon rack that holds twelve spoons. The maker is unknown. 13" high x 24" wide. ($75+).

102

Right:
Pyrography was also popular as a way to apply a design to other materials besides wood. This advertisement from Thayer & Chandler in Chicago appeared in *The Cosmopolitan* magazine in the early 1900s. The ad offered a "Naan Plush" pillow top stamped with a Gibson Girl design ready for burning for only 35¢. A company catalog was available which illustrated 1,000 designs stamped on articles of Naan Plush, wood, or leather.

Left:
Wastebasket made in sections and laced together. The basket is decorated on all sides with flowers. 13" high. ($60+).

Leather "hand burnt" pillow slip similar to the ones advertised in the Montgomery Ward catalog circa 1916. Although the catalog examples were decorated with other designs, they were finished with fringe and leather lacing around the edges as this one is. A Gibson Girl provides the inspiration for this pillow. *Courtesy of Grand Lake Historical Society, Grand Lake, Colorado.*

Large pyrography lidded baby chest featuring a stork and flower decoration. Pieces as large as this one are very hard to find. 13.5" high x 26.5" wide x 15" deep. ($125).

HUMMINGBIRD

Above:
A more recent type of wood burnt plaque features two hummingbirds as well as flowers. Size 6" wide x 8" tall. ($10).

Above right:
Wood souvenirs circa 1930s and 1940s were produced in great numbers using simpler burnt wood decorations. Many of them featured unique designs and a collection of these items can be assembled inexpensively to be displayed on a small wall shelf unit. Pictured is a box with drawer marked "Maryville, Mo," a cigarette box from Cleveland, Ohio (featuring a Scotty dog similar to one owned by President Roosevelt at the time), a sailboat thermometer from Morganton, N.C., a canoe from Lawton, Okla., and a pine tree thermometer. ($10-$12 each).

Right:
A collection of pyrography pieces is displayed on two open shelves. Items include boxes, plaques, picture frames, and a book rack.

Souvenirs

Tablecloths, head scarves, and handkerchiefs decorated with state maps were produced as souvenirs during the 1950s. These handkerchiefs can be used to make colorful pillow tops as pictured here. Nearly all of these handkerchiefs were made of cotton. Many were manufactured in the Philippines. These examples feature maps of California (2), Florida, and New Jersey. Most of the handkerchiefs measure 12" or 13" square. (Handkerchiefs, $10 each).

Since the early part of the twentieth century, any location that catered to tourists also supplied souvenirs. Many of these items can give a cabin of today an interesting and distinct personality. In the early years, postcards, glass cups, china plates, and pennants were all popular. Other china souvenir pieces included cups and saucers, bowls, and pin trays. Much of this china was imported from Germany, England, or Austria. These items were all popular circa 1890s to the beginning of World War I. One of the co-author's father and his parents traveled extensively by train during those years. Each trip added several new pennants to a collection that eventually became a top for a new comfort.

Sterling silver souvenir spoons were also popular with long ago travelers from the 1890s through the 1920s. For current collectors, spoons with figural handles featuring Indians are especially desirable. Spoons representing favorite places are often preferred by cabin owners.

As the National Parks and surrounding areas were developed to accommodate guests, new souvenirs were produced to be sold to these visitors. Besides paper products (See Paper Collectibles chapter), pennants, plates, cups, leather goods, wood products, and Indian made rugs, pottery, and baskets were all sold in gift shops close to many of the National Parks.

As the decades passed, a need was found and filled for cheaper souvenirs. With the advance and convenience of automobile travel, more families took vacations, but unlike the earlier travelers, many of these new tourists were on budgets. The souvenirs made of wood with bark still attached, the small birch canoes, Indian dolls, and various "mailers" helped fill this niche. (See Indian Connection chapter.) All of the wood souvenirs of this type are still readily available at reasonable prices and can be used in cabin decorating. Whether a collection is made of only salt and pepper shakers, wood plaques, or a variety of items, it would be easy to assemble.

Tourists traditionally return from a trip loaded with postcards and brochures. These items add color to a cabin's décor when they are displayed in bulk in a picnic basket or suitcase or even under glass on a coffee table. They also offer reminders of past trips, perhaps from long ago.

In the early years, stereoscopic view cards (Paper Collectibles chapter) could be purchased picturing various tourist sites. By the 1940s, many of the same tourist attractions were being featured on View-Master reels, which also gave the viewer a 3-D effect. These reels could be purchased while on a trip or ordered from a catalog after the traveler returned home. Early reels are especially appealing for cabin owners if their own area, such as a nearby National Park or town, is pictured.

During the 1950s, an interesting phenomenon developed in the textile industry. Tablecloths and tea (dish) towels were produced using maps of different states as the decoration. Although map tablecloths of many states were manufactured, the most abundant ones found today represent California, Florida, and Texas. Because these souvenirs are so colorful, they can be hung on a wall, used on a table in the kitchen or on a porch to add color to the area. The towels can also be hung on the wall or utilized for their intended purpose.

Following the success of souvenir tablecloths, handkerchiefs and head scarves were also produced decorated with maps of different states. Scarves can be displayed individually or mounted on a wall as a group by hanging them on pegs, while the handkerchiefs make colorful pillow tops.

State plates can also be found which feature maps as part of their designs, but most of the plates picture familiar places located in the states. These plates have been made for decades and are very colorful when several are hung on a wall. Since they have been produced for so many years, a collection of plates representing the cabin's home state might be fun to accumulate.

Pillowcases made of rayon or satin were sold as souvenir items as early as the years of World War I. War-related WWII souvenir pillow cases were also produced. Many of these items were printed bearing the name of a military base, "Mother" or "Sweetheart," but these inexpensive souvenirs were also manufactured which featured state, city, and National Park names and designs. (*See Camp Blankets, Quilts, and Comforts chapter.*)

Decks of cards have also remained a staple of the souvenir industry for decades. The most interesting are those which picture scenes from the area they represent. Vintage playing cards provide a unique collectible because they can actually be used when card games are played at the cabin.

When accumulating souvenirs to be used in decorating a cabin, the final results will be more meaningful if a family's own vintage souvenirs are included. Older pieces originally sold close to the cabin's location also add a personal touch.

Many souvenirs available to resort visitors in the early 1900s were quite elaborate when compared to today's standards. They included hand painted plates, cups, and pitchers as well as fancy glass pieces. The souvenirs reflected the style of the times when hand painted plates were used on plate rails in dining rooms and glass fronted china cabinets were filled with beautiful china and glassware from the period. Pictured are two of these types of souvenirs from the resort town of Eureka Springs, Arkansas. The hand painted plate shows the Basin Park Hotel, which was built in 1905. Since the scene pictures both a horse drawn vehicle and early automobiles, it is probably circa 1914. The printing on the back reads "DESIGNED AND HAND PAINTED/FOR/SMITH BROS./EUREKA SPRINGS, ARK." The plate is also marked "GERMANY." The fancy glass cup has been decorated with red and "Eureka Springs, Ark" is spelled out across the top. (Plate $100+; cup $40-$50).

Sterling silver state souvenir spoons were advertised in this circa 1916 Montgomery Ward catalog. Two designs were offered. The "cut-out" spoons sold for $1.08 each while the more traditional state spoons were priced at 76¢ each. Sterling spoons were popular both as souvenirs and because of their variety during this period.

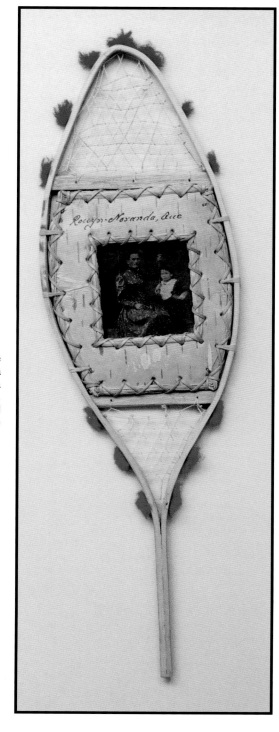

Unusual Indian made miniature snowshoe apparently used for a souvenir from Quebec, Canada during the early part of the century. It holds a picture of a woman and child. ($95) *Courtesy of Avalanche Ranch, Redstone, Colorado.*

Souvenir spoons have been sold which represent states, National Parks, and other tourist attractions for over one hundred years. The most desirable spoons for today's collector are the ones made of sterling silver. Silverplate spoons were produced in later years and the more recent spoons are made of even cheaper materials. The three sterling silver spoons pictured are all from Colorado and depict Rocky Mountain National Park, the state of Colorado, and Grand Lake, Colorado. ($20-$30 each). Souvenir spoons can be found which represent all fifty states.

Colorful new pillow made from four old felt pennants. Table coverings and comfort tops can also be produced by sewing pennants together in interesting designs. ($100+). *Courtesy of Avalanche Ranch, Redstone, Colorado.*

As the years passed, souvenirs became more affordable for the general public to buy. Decorated felt pennants were inexpensive and could be found at most popular tourist destinations. They were not breakable and did not take up much space in a suitcase which was a plus for those travelers making their trip by train. This type of souvenir has been produced for over seventy-five years. The early felt ones, decorated with Indians, are especially collectible. Shown is an interesting display of pennants of all sizes and from many different places. Included are examples from Milwaukee, Wisconsin, Rocky Mountain National Park, Grand Canyon National Park, Cheyenne, Wyoming, Pikes Peak Region, Grand Lake, Colorado, Leadville, Colorado, Greeley, Colorado, and Royal Gorge Bridge near Colorado Springs. The prices are determined by age, size, condition, design, and the popularity of the place represented. ($15-$30 each).

Pennants representing National Parks have always been popular. This one from Yellowstone Park, circa 1960s, is decorated with a bear as well as park scenes. ($15+). Also shown is a molded plaque or plate circa 1950s to 1960s that could be hung on the wall. It pictures Old Faithful, Great Falls, and the Fishing Bridge along with a bear. Marked on the back is "Copyright HH TAMMEN/MADE IN USA/GENUINE PRESSE WOOD." ($15-$20) A leather Yellowstone Park photo album is also pictured. It is marked "All I Did Was Hug a Little." ($15-$18).

A collection of souvenirs from Rocky Mountain National Park in Colorado. Included are a pennant circa 1950s to 1960s, ($15+); a decal that could be placed on a suitcase or car window ($8); a plate and postcard picturing the gift shop located on Trail Ridge Road in the park; and two early park pamphlets. The plate is marked "The Fall River Pass Store is an interesting place along/Trail Ridge Road in Rocky Mountain National Park/The drive between Estes Park and Grand Lake over/Trail Ridge reached an altitude of 12,213 feet,/ is one of America's most scenic drives./MADE IN STAFFORDSHIRE ENGLAND/IMPORTED EXCLUSIVELY FOR/ROCKY MOUNTAIN MOTOR CO/ROCKY MOUNTAIN NATIONAL PARK/ESTES PARK, COLORADO." Plate: "Old English Staffordshire Ware/ JONROTH/ENGLAND" ($20). The larger pamphlet circa 1934 is marked "ROCKY MOUNTAIN/NATIONAL PARK/ COLORADO/UNITED STATES DEPARTMENT OF THE INTERIOR/NATIONAL PARK SERVICE" ($8-$10). The smaller pamphlet is marked "1948/VACATION TOURS BY BUS/Including/Transportation, Meals and Lodging/Via/ Rocky Mountain National Park,/Estes Park and Grand Lake,/Colorado." ($3-$5).

A vintage National Park Service ranger hat could also be displayed as part of a National Park collection. The headband on this example reads "USNPS." The inside label reads "Gregory's Uniform Specialists/Greeley, Colo." The Park Service hat came in a holder that can be hung on a cabin wall. ($35+).

This old wood stein represents another type of souvenir that was sold to tourists in the early part of the 20th century. It is marked "Rye Beach New York." It is a very early example of the later inexpensive souvenirs of this type. *From the collection of Bob Scott.* Not enough examples to determine a price.

Inexpensive souvenirs made of wood with bark still visible continued to be made for decades. The same items were sold in different locations with the insignia changed to fit various tourist destinations. Pictured are a jug, candlesticks, six pairs of salt and pepper shakers, thermometer, bank, pen and ink well, and napkin and key holders. ($10-$20 each).

Three larger wood products made of wood and bark. (Covered canister, $20-$25; candle holders, $8-$10; and pail with handle, $15).

Through the years every family collects an assortment of postcard folders, brochures, and booklets from various vacations. These souvenirs can make a colorful decorating arrangement for a new or old cabin. At the same time, the items bring back fond memories of trips from long ago. These souvenirs are displayed in a metal green picnic basket. (Picnic basket, $40+; brochures and booklets, $3-$10 each).

Two types of plaques were also made as part of the wood-bark souvenir line. They included those finished with poems or sayings and the ones which featured scenery pictures from a tourist destination. The scenery plaques are still sold as souvenirs today. A collection of these plaques makes an interesting wall arrangement, perhaps in a cabin bathroom. The pictured plaques come from Yellowstone National Park, Grand Lake, Colorado, Maine, Little Brown Church in the Vale, Nashua, Iowa, and Steamboat Springs, Colorado. ($8-$18 each).

Many practical items have been turned into souvenirs with the addition of a metal tag or printed label. This cigarette case is an example. With the enhancement of a decorative metal shield which features a lake and mountain scene and "Adirondack Mts." the hammered copper case is transformed into a souvenir from the Adirondacks. ($35).

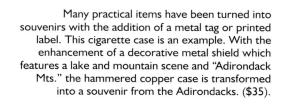

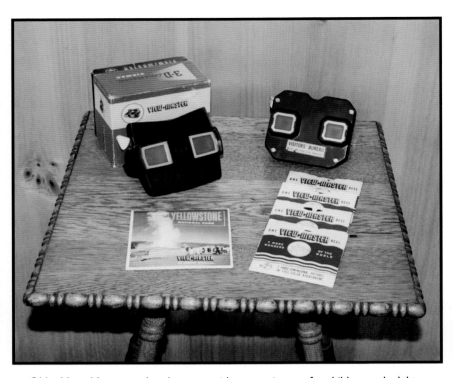

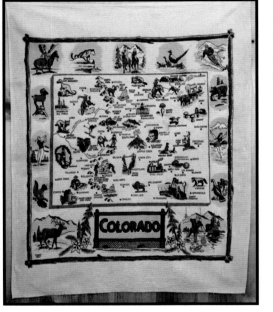

Older View-Masters and reels can provide entertainment for children and adults alike when reels of the area surrounding a cabin are available for browsing. Two different models of View-Masters are pictured along with travel reels that could be used with them. One of the View-Masters came in a plastic box marked "View-Master" that allowed space inside for both the View-Master and extra reels. Both View-Masters are marked "Sawyer's View-Master/Portland Ore." The box for the other View-Master is marked "Model E./3-Dimension Viewer." The reels picture Yellowstone National Park, copyright 1962, and Rocky Mountain Park, copyright 1949. (View-Master and three Yellowstone reels, $18-$20; five Colorado reels from 1940s, $9 set; older View-Master in plastic box, $15).

Souvenir tablecloths decorated with state maps were popular in the 1950s. These colorful accents can be used on a kitchen table or hung on the wall. This Colorado example is smaller than most of the cloths and makes a nice wall decoration. 31" wide x 39" long. It is marked "An Original/YUCCA/PRINT." ($40+).

This larger California cloth apparently has never been used. It is 45" wide x 52" long. These colorful tablecloths picture many of the tourist attractions in the states at the time they were produced. This cloth adds color to an antique round oak table and chairs. The seats of the mission oak chairs have been covered with cowhide. Colorful Harlequin dishes produced by the Homer Laughlin Co. from 1938 to 1964 are featured on the table. (Tablecloth, $50).

Besides tablecloths and tea towels, souvenir head scarves were also manufactured during the 1950s, 1960s, and early 1970s decorated with maps of various states. Since these scarves are smaller than tablecloths, they are easier to display as a collection. Five of these scarves are pictured hanging on pegs. Included are examples from Oregon, California, Arizona, and Colorado. These scarves are made of satin or rayon. (In very good condition, $15-$25 each, depending on popularity of the state).

Large cities or famous tourist attractions also arranged to have head scarves made to promote their areas. Las Vegas scarves are particularly popular because they picture earlier casinos that have since been razed to make way for larger properties. Other Las Vegas souvenirs pictured include a linen postcard from the Hotel Thunderbird with a postmark of 1952, a deck of cards from the Frontier Hotel as well as Thunderbird and Plaza matchbook covers which were kept as souvenirs. The Las Vegas linen postcard folder features postcards of the city as well as the Golden Nugget Gambling Hall, Hotel Sahara, Thunderbird Hotel, Desert Inn, Flamingo Hotel, Sands Hotel, and Last Frontier Hotel. (Scarf, $25; postcard folder, $10; deck of cards, $5-$10; matchbook covers, $3-$5 each; single postcard, $3).

Left:
In addition to tablecloths, tea towels were also produced decorated with maps of various states. This never-used souvenir represents Florida. These towels are small enough they could be framed for a wall hanging or displayed on a towel rack. ($15-$20).

Souvenir playing cards can be both collectible and useful for cabin owners. Playing cards are available that promote a tourist attraction, such as Universal Studios, National Parks, or individual states. In addition, many vintage decks of cards were produced with appropriate pictures that would be fun to use for cabin card games for both family and friends. Appropriate cards include double decks featuring ducks ($5-$7), fish and deer ($5-$7), and two different styles of sailboats ($12-$15). The duck and sailboat cards were produced by Congress and the deer and fishing cards were given away as advertising for "W.J. Bullock, Inc of Fairfield, Ala." The joker card is marked "Redislip."

Before the arrival of Disneyland, Knott's Berry Farm in Buena Park, California, was among the most popular of Southern California's tourist destinations. This head scarf pictures many things for visitors to see and do at the farm. The souvenirs displayed on the scarf came from a family trip taken by one of the authors in 1953. They include a lidded box marked "KNOTTS BERRY FARM/ CALIFORNIA." The top is decorated with a raised design of a covered wagon. It was produced using a pressed composition-type material made to resemble wood. Each card in the Knott's Berry Farm deck of cards features a photograph taken at various locations at the park. The Steak House menu gives a history of the farm which began in the 1920s as a berry farm which sold berries to people traveling along the road. The enterprise began to grow and by the 1950s, the combined seating for all the restaurants was 1,575. This menu offered a New York cut steak served with soup, green salad, hot rolls, sherbet, vegetable, potato, and coffee for $2.75. A pioneer beef stew with green salad, hot rolls, and coffee could be ordered for $1.00.

State plates have been sold as souvenirs for decades. All of the plates feature pictures of famous state landmarks. Some plates use a map decoration to identify important places while others offer illustrations in a pleasing design. These vintage souvenirs are very inexpensive and a collector could decorate a wall with plates representing favorite past vacation destinations. The Texas plate is marked on the back "BANDO/Golden Stone/Microwave-Safe/ KOREA; the Iowa plate is unmarked. ($5-$8 each).

This unused scrapbook could be used to mount vintage photographs of early camping and cabin life as well as hunting and fishing trips. ($35).

Later postcards from the 1930s and 1940s have recently gained popularity with cabin owners. Called "linen" postcards, these items are very colorful and a group of these "folders" can be framed and used as a colorful wall decoration. This type of postcard was only produced in America.

The later "chrome" postcards are not yet very collectible, perhaps because even those from the 1960s look very much like the postcards produced today.

Although harder to find, cards to be used with stereoscopes offer another interesting cabin collectible. These cards provide photographs of early tourist attractions as well as cards picturing hunting, fishing, and other sporting activities. When used with an old stereoscope, the view can be seen in 3-D. These sets were sold for decades in the early part of the 19th century and were still available as late as the early 1930s. These view cards can be much more expensive than the old postcards when they represent unusual or scarce subjects. Many more scenery postcards were produced than stereoscopic cards picturing the same areas, so some stereoscopic cards may cost $30 or more. Those showing more frequently photographed views can be purchased for $5.00 to $8.00 each. Children and adults alike can be entertained by using old stereoscope viewers and cards to see how areas have changed since the early days.

Old photographs and cameras also are becoming more popular for use in cabin décor. The most appealing are vintage photos that have some meaning for the cabin owners. With the current commercial photo equipment available, these pictures can be enlarged, matted, and framed even when negatives are not available. Old sports pictures are especially desirable. If family photographs are not available, vintage albums can sometimes be found which contain usable pictures. Especially interesting are the ones that feature old bathing suits, camping trips, hunting and fishing trips, lodges, and identified early scenery pictures. These photos can be placed under glass on a coffee or dining table, enlarged and framed to be hung on a wall, placed on tables, or collected and mounted in an old scrapbook.

Other vintage paper collectibles that add interest to a new or old cabin include booklets, brochures, menus, newspapers, and road maps collected from family vacations or picturing the area of the cabin's location. Old menus from area restaurants are especially appealing because the prices listed are so inexpensive; it is hard for even adults to remember those "good old days." A glass-

Paper collectibles that are appropriate to be used in cabin décor are relatively inexpensive and can be tied to a cabin family's interest or location.

Postcards offer the widest selection of views since they have been produced for over one hundred years. The early hand-colored examples are the most expensive, but these cards can be matted and framed to make nice wall decorations. Currently some firms will enlarge and mat an individual's treasured postcards so the originals can be carefully protected in an acid free box or album. Early postcards of interest include those of "Indian Maidens," *(See Indian Connection chapter),* old lodges (especially if they picture the rustic furniture used in furnishings), and early Adirondack "Camps." Each cabin owner will want to pursue his or her own interest in the postcard collecting field. Surely early local postcards would also warrant attention along with those representing fishing, hunting, sailing, or other sports popular in the area.

topped table could be used to display a collection of menus to show the costs of the items listed. A rack of old maps can also offer a hint of nostalgia when they can be marked with the highways traveled from past vacations. Any map showing the old Route 66 is particularly popular for today's collector. During the 1950s, Conoco not only provided travelers with maps for a trip, but the company would send the traveler a booklet containing information about sights to see on the vacation and motels or hotels where families or individuals could stay. *(See also Souvenirs chapter.)*

Since postcard albums, scrapbooks, and stereoscopic card boxes don't take up much space, these items can be stored in stacked suitcases or vintage picnic baskets to allow easy access when needed. Family photographs can also be stored in these types of containers so they are easily accessible for browsing.

Paper collectibles can be enjoyed and accumulated over the years and provide unique conversation pieces for both visitors and owners.

Postcard from Adirondack Inn, Sacandaga Park, New York, mailed in 1907. It was made in Germany for "Frank A. Hamwey, Sacandaga Park, N.Y." Postcards from the Adirondacks are especially popular with collectors. ($8 with some wear).

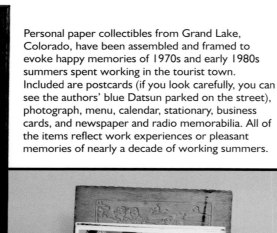

Personal paper collectibles from Grand Lake, Colorado, have been assembled and framed to evoke happy memories of 1970s and early 1980s summers spent working in the tourist town. Included are postcards (if you look carefully, you can see the authors' blue Datsun parked on the street), photograph, menu, calendar, stationary, business cards, and newspaper and radio memorabilia. All of the items reflect work experiences or pleasant memories of nearly a decade of working summers.

This postcard, also produced in Germany, is labeled "Adirondack Mountains. A Private Camp." It was mailed in 1905. Pictured is a log structure on the shore along with a canoe and dock. ($8-$10).

Postcards offer one of the easiest methods of documenting "how things used to be." A nice collection can be stored in a pyrography wood postcard box as shown. These cards date mostly from the early 1900s. (Postcard box, $50).

No. 165   ENTRANCE OLD FAITHFUL INN — YELLOWSTONE PARK.   HAYNES-PHOTO.   Printed in Germany.

Vintage postcards featuring the buildings in the National Parks add interest to a cabin postcard collection. Pictured is the Old Faithful Inn at Yellowstone National Park. It is labeled "Haynes Photo Made in Germany." The Inn was built in 1904. ($6-$8).

23440.   OLD FAITHFUL INN DINING ROOM, YELLOWSTONE PARK

Old Faithful Inn Dining Room at Yellowstone, circa 1920. The room is furnished with Old Hickory chairs, rustic light fixtures, and a stone fireplace. Many of the chairs are still in use today. The card is marked "Published by J.E. Haynes, St. Paul Minn. Official Photographer Yellowstone National Park." ($8-$10).

12538.   FIREPLACE AND STAIRWAY IN LOBBY, OLD FAITHFUL INN, YELLOWSTONE PARK.   COPR. DETROIT PUBLISHING CO.

The lobby of the Old Faithful Inn featured fine Indian rugs, a large stone fireplace, log walls, and a rustic décor. This vintage card is marked "PHOSTINT Card Made only by Detroit Pub Co." ($8-$10).

23559.   CANYON CAMP LODGE INTERIOR, YELLOWSTONE PARK.   HAYNES-PHOTO.

A room at the Canyon Camp Lodge at Yellowstone, circa 1920s. The furnishings include a wood stove, teakettle, pitcher and bowl, slop bucket, candle, table, chair, and bed. Card marked "Published by J.E. Haynes, St. Paul Minn. Official Photographer, Yellowstone National Park." ($5-$8).

15378. Grand Lake Lodge
Rocky Mountain National Park

Grand Lake Lodge, circa 1920s, which is adjacent to the western entrance of Rocky Mountain National Park. The lodge is still in operation today and its vintage cabins are rented nightly during the season. ($8-$10).

FIREPLACE AND CORNER OF THE DINING ROOM · GRAND LAKE, COLO.

The dining room of Grand Lake Lodge was also furnished with Old Hickory chairs. Postcard, circa 1940s. ($8-$10).

"Hand Colored" postcard (postmarked 1929) pictures the lobby of Colorado's Grand Lake Lodge. The card was published by F. P. Clatworthy, Estes Park, Colorado. The rustic lobby was furnished with a variety of Old Hickory rockers, a circular fireplace, Indian rugs, and taxidermy pieces. Most of this furniture is still in use at the lodge today. Because of a fire in 1973, the woven seats and backs have been replaced. ($20-$25).

Framed collection of "linen" postcard folders representing different areas of the country. These later cards (circa 1930s and 1940s) offer a colorful accent when used in cabin decorating. (Folders, $4-$8 each).

A stereoscope and view cards were still being offered for sale as late as 1931 as this advertisement shows. It was featured in the Sears Fall and Winter catalog for 1931-1932. The stereoscope sold for $1.00 while a box of one hundred views was priced at only 98¢. Both prices were considerably lower than the earlier years and perhaps old stock was being disposed of.

Stereoscopic card picturing the Mount of the Holy Cross near Minturn, Colorado. On the back is listed a series of forty-three Colorado views available from the unknown firm. Most of the views were from Colorado railroads. ($8-$10).

Stereoscopes and their stereoscopic cards offer a more unusual method of remembering the past. These products were sold for several decades at the beginning of the 20th century. Cards were produced which pictured many tourist attractions as well as hunting and fishing, and other sporting activities. When viewed, the pictures took on a three-dimension effect. Pictured are a stereoscope, stereoscopic cards, and their box. A Grand Canyon National Park pennant is in the background. (Stereoscope, $75-$100; cards, $2-$10 each; empty box, $5-$8; pennant, $15).

Two different styled stereo cards picturing hunting scenes. One reads "Two Days' Sport. 198 Black Ducks Hung Up. 1898 T.W. Ingersoll." The other is labeled only "464. Quail Hunter's Lunch in the Woods." ($8-$10 each).

Old cameras and photographs can also remind cabin owners and visitors how it used to be. Pictured are framed vintage photographs which show camping scenes. The two cameras were both made by Kodak. The Kodak Junior (Six-16 Series II, f6.3 lens) was produced by the Eastman Kodak Company in Rochester, New York, circa mid to late 1930s. It still has its original box and booklet ($25 to $30). The Kodak "Brownie Junior" box camera is the Six-20 model and probably dates from the 1940s. ($12-$15).

Fishing scenes were also reproduced in stereo cards. These three cards include a man and woman "landing a small mouth bass" (1903), a trout fisherman, and a woman fishing along a bank (notice her fishing creel prominently displayed). ($8-$10 each).

The Kodak Junior Six-16 with the f6.3 lens was advertised in the Sears Fall and Winter catalog for 1935-36. It sold for $13.95, rather an expensive price for the depression years. The cheaper model could be purchased for $8.95.

This circa 1920 bathing beauty not only wears her swimming suit, but a head covering, belt, rolled-down stockings and shoes (probably made of rubber). It is photographs like this one that are fun to find even when the subject is unknown. ($15+).

Old photographs offer a variety of subjects that can be used to enhance cabin décor. Family pictures are especially desirable. Pictured are three old sports team photographs from Neodesha High School in Neodesha, Kansas in 1922 and 1923. The authors' father-grandfather was a player on these football and basketball teams.

Males also willingly posed for swimming pictures. This unknown subject wears his two-piece suit, but he has his hat handy, maybe to ward off sunburn, circa 1920. ($3-$5).

Vintage camping photos are especially appealing. These folks appear to have set up housekeeping in the yard, perhaps for a family reunion. Shelves stocked with supplies lean against the tree, regular chairs have been carried from the house to use for seating and sunbonnets appear to be the fashion of the day. The photograph was found in a small photo album filled with vintage pictures circa 1915. (Album, $25+).

Leather "Snaps and Scraps" photo album marked "Blue Mt. Lake, N.Y. Adirondack Mts." The album is filled with photographs from a summer trip to the area in July 1940. ($35-$40).

Early photograph of a distant relative of the authors' family following a successful day of hunting. Unlike today, many men in the early part of the 20th century needed to hunt to supply food for their families. Other photographs in this old family album picture heavy snowfalls and impassable roads. Circa 1920s.

Family photographs provide the nicest memories and for cabin owners who are fortunate enough to have retained their family albums, photos from this source can be used to add a personal touch. Photographs can be enlarged, using the commercial photo machines, matted, and framed to be hung on a cabin wall or mounted in small frames to be used as table accents. Pictured is one of the co-authors and her father and mother on a 1938 fishing vacation to the Missouri Ozarks. Fish were caught as shown in the photo, so the trip proved successful.

Souvenir covered wagon lamp, 7" long x 5.5" high. These types of small lamps were sold in gift shops in tourist towns for many years. Pictured on one side of the wagon is a mountain scene, and two fawns are shown in the other picture. Similar covered wagons were also sold in kit form, to be assembled by the buyer. ($20-$25). Two vintage brochures are also pictured. They are both from Grand Lake, Colorado (circa 1950s and 1960s), which is located at the west entrance to Rocky Mountain National Park. ($6-$8).

Early maps of favorite states or locations can also add interesting touches to cabin décor. Pictured is a "Directory: Rocky Mountain Region Colorado, Wyoming and New Mexico." It includes "Official Tourist Information." The booklet was produced by the Highway Publishing Company of Denver, Colorado in 1929. It includes a hotel directory, cottage camp directory, maps, photographs, information, and many advertisements which picture business establishments of the era. ($35+).

Two vintage menus also from Grand Lake, Colorado, circa 1950s. The Pine Cone Inn offered a cheeseburger for 25¢ while a five-course dinner of chicken or trout could be ordered for $1.00. The Corner Cupboard's dinners were priced from 85¢ to $1.50 each. Desserts included pie for 15¢, sodas for 15¢, sundaes for 20¢, and banana splits, 25¢. Cheeseburgers could be purchased for 30¢. Old menus from favorite locations can be displayed in a rack or matted and framed and used for wall decoration. ($10-$18+).

Colorful road maps can also be used as accessories in a cabin. With the current interest in the old Route 66 Highway, maps which traced this famous highway are particularly collectible. The Standard Oil Co. Southwestern United States map from the early 1950s features this highway. The vintage map also includes markings from the co-author's trips during the early 1950s with overnight stays indicated. The Iowa Shell map dates from the 1930s and includes a radio log so tourists could listen to favorite radio programs as they traveled from their home territory. The Colorado Skelly Oil Company map dates from the 1940s and offers a central states mileage chart as well as maps. The Kansas map issued by Sinclair, also from the 1940s, includes a "pictorial sight-seeing guide" as well as highway maps. Thirty pictures of Kansas highlights are printed on the back of the map. The Philips 66 1950s Nebraska map reminds motorists of the 65-mile speed limit during the day and 55-mile limit after dark. Conoco was responsible for the "touraide map" of Wyoming printed in the 1960s. On the back of the map, 22 "touraide attractions" in the state are listed and described. It is surprising how much information was included in the highway maps of earlier years. The most surprising thing of all is that each of the pictured maps was given away free to gasoline station customers. (Maps, $2-$20 each, depending on age and interest.)

Vintage oak suitcase (perhaps one used to hold salesman samples) makes a good display venue for a variety of paper collectibles. Included are postcard folders of Hoover Dam, White Mountains and Grand Canyon, matchbooks from various clubs in Reno and Las Vegas, Nevada as well as Gene Autry Hotels and Fred Harvey Restaurants, and miniature playing cards from Texas and the Grand Canyon. Also included in the display are several vintage road maps, a "Touraide" specialty prepared by Conoco for the co-author's family vacation in 1954, and vintage brochures for Yellowstone National Park, Central City, Colorado, and the Carlsbad Caverns. An old picnic basket could also be used to display these types of souvenirs.

A vintage collection of travel decals can be assembled to be used to decorate an old set of luggage. The suitcases can then be stacked and displayed. The arrangement of colorful labels would also make an interesting "picture" when framed and mounted on a cabin wall, perhaps in conjunction with framed linen type postcard folders. Tourist towns and National Parks have sold these type souvenirs for decades. Examples from past family vacation spots would be of special interest. ($7-$15 each).

Sports Related Accessories

Sports is surely the one category of collectibles that every cabin owner can find something to identify with. The field is so vast because it includes both individual and team sports. Cabins tend to be built in places that encourage these activities. Summer cabins located near lakes provide opportunities for boating and sailing as well as fishing and swimming. *(See Fishing and Hunting Collectibles chapter.)* Most of the resort areas in a cabin's vicinity provide golf and tennis amenities as well. Cabins that were primarily built to take advantage of winter locations usually were built with skiing in mind. In addition, ice skating, snowshoeing, and sledding activities can also be found in the same area.

Whether it is summer or winter sports that appeal to cabin owners, collectibles from their favorite activities can add a personal touch to the décor of a vacation home.

Swimming has been included as a summer cabin activity since the early days of the 1900s. Early examples of both men's and women's bathing attire can make an interesting cabin wall display. Old magazine covers and vintage photographs picturing long ago swimmers can be framed and added to a summer cabin wall to contrast with the styles of today's water enthusiasts. Boating and sailing have also provided cabin owners with many pleasurable memories for more than a century. For those who prefer a faster ride, a boat with an attached motor has offered another form of recreation since the first such motor was patented by Evinrude in 1911. By 1922, Christopher Smith began the Chris-Craft Boats firm, which produced some of the finest boats of their type ever made. Vintage photographs of these early sailboats and pleasure boats, especially if they have some kind of family connection, can also be used to decorate cabin walls.

These early Indian made ladies snowshoes with red tassels and leather bindings are pictured in a pack basket which retains its original canvas covering. This display would work well beside a cabin fireplace. Indian snowshoes decorated with yarn are the most desirable examples because of the added color and extra craftsmanship. The canvas covered pack basket is also more unique than the more usual pack baskets. (Pair of snowshoes, $325; canvas covered pack basket, $395). *Courtesy of Avalanche Ranch, Redstone, Colorado.*

Toys representing these types of water craft can be collected to be displayed on a shelf or table top. Items featuring vintage sailing or motor boat images can also be used for cabin accents. Bookends, lamps, drinking glasses, or dishes are especially appealing. According to a listing in *Cabin Life* from Feb./March 2003, Ralph Samuelson built the first water skis in 1922 and used them as he was towed behind a motor powered boat. The sport didn't catch on until much later, however. By the 1950s, the water skiing sport was so popular that enthusiasts made frequent trips every summer, hauling their boats and equipment, to reach suitable lakes to practice their skills. For cabin owners who remember those days and perhaps still own some of the early skis, these items can be put to new use as cabin accessories. The skis can be mounted on a cabin wall as part of a larger arrangement or crossed like snow skis to fill a smaller space. Likewise, a vintage collection of the once popular bathing caps could also be displayed in a summer cabin. They can be placed on simple styrofoam molds on a shelf or table top or hung on a wall. A large variety of these caps were produced for decades including those made in different colors or decorated with flowers. Several of these caps hung on pegs in a bathroom would also add an interesting touch.

Vintage magazine covers or old calendars featuring a variety of sports are readily available for framing and a whole wall of a cabin could be enlivened with such items. Examples that are especially interesting and collectible are those from the early 1900s, which feature women participating in various sports, since female participants were infrequent in those times.

Vintage golf and tennis equipment also offer interesting collectibles that can be used in cabin décor. The early wood handled golf clubs are especially attractive. They can be displayed in a vintage golf bag, mounted on the wall, or professionally framed in a glass fronted case along with other golf memorabilia such as a paper program, golf trophy, and perhaps an early photograph of a golfer. In addition, old golf related clothing has recently become a popular sports collectible, which could be featured in a wall arrangement. Vintage tennis rackets can also be used, perhaps as part of a display, which includes golf memorabilia. Tennis rackets are easy to mount on a wall and a collection of six or eight rackets from various companies and time periods would add an interesting cabin wall display for a collector who loves the game of tennis.

For those owners of a summer cabin who enjoy more passive forms of recreation, various vintage sets of croquet could add a nostalgic touch to a porch or deck. If surrounding space is available, the croquet sets can also be put to use. The nice thing about croquet is that it can be played by all ages and the basic game can be learned quickly so it makes a nice ice breaker.

Cabins that were primarily built to take advantage of winter sports can be enlivened with collectible items relating to these cold weather activities. The most popular of these collectibles used for interior decorating is the snowshoe. Snowshoes can be displayed in pack baskets, leaned against a fireplace, or mounted on cabin walls in a variety of ways. The Indian-made shoes are the most collectible and therefore the most expensive. These snowshoes often were finished with yarn and this adds touches of color to an arrangement. Snowshoes can be found in all sizes so an interesting wall display can be made using a variety of snowshoe sizes and styles.

Although skiing was not yet popular in the United States during the early 1900s, Corinne Humphrey in her article "High Style Ski" for *Log Home Living* gives information that Christian Lund of Norway founded the Northland Ski Co. in St. Paul, Minnesota in 1911. By 1912 the Bass Co. of Maine was also making skis. More U.S. firms began producing skis as the decades passed, but it wasn't until the 1932 Olympics held in Lake Placid, New York, that skiing became a popular sport in the United States. The skiing phenomenon continued to grow as more and more ski resorts were opened after World War II. Many of these new enterprises were established by veterans of the Army's 10th Mountain Division who trained as skiers in World War II.

Because of the sport's popularity, vintage wood skis are in demand as accessories to be used in adding a nostalgic touch to a winter cabin. Bamboo ski poles also make interesting collectibles. Skis can be placed beside a fireplace, hung on a cabin wall or above a door opening (in a crossed position), or several sets of skis and poles can be placed in a wood barrel. If space is available, a wall arrangement, which includes a collection of both skis and snowshoes, can be assembled. Vintage ski posters can be used as part of such an arrangement or several could be framed and displayed together. While older ski clothing is harder to find, these items, particularly boots, sweaters, or hats, would add additional interest to the décor of a ski retreat. Such clothing could be hung on pegs in an entry hall or combined with skis for a wall arrangement.

Ice skates, too, can add interest to a winter cabin. The easiest way to display these nostalgic collectibles is to hang the skates on a rustic coat rack. Older skates were made of wood or metal to be clamped to the skater's shoes. A variety of these types of skates are readily available to use in decorating. Other vintage skates can be found attached to shoes or boots similar to the ones used today. Original boxes can add color to an arrangement of skates displayed on a shelf. To give a display added interest, skates can be shown which feature a past Olympic ice skating champion's name on a box or skates. Several Olympic winners endorsed skates for various companies, which then featured the personality in advertisements for their products.

In addition to skiing, snowshoeing, and skating, nearly everyone has had the pleasure of sledding during their younger days. Whether it was on a snowy hill in some small town, or in an organized commercial setting, the pleasant memories are much the same. For this reason, vintage sleds are also in demand for use in decorating a winter cabin. Sleds can be attractive accessories whether they are the old wooden sleds from the early 1900s or a Flexible Flyer model of more recent vintage. S.L. Allen & Co. of Philadelphia began production of the Flexible Flyer sleds during the early 1900s and the sleds were made using the Flexible Flyer name until 1996. Push sleds used in winter, mainly to replace a baby buggy or stroller, also provide interesting cabin accessories. The sleds can be used to hold a collection of ice skates, wrapped Christmas gifts in December, or a variety of appropriate pillows.

Winter toys can also offer interesting collectibles to be used to enliven cabin décor. Lithographed tin ski toys, vintage dolls in their original ice skating or ski costumes, children's skis or snowshoes, and plastic snowmen are especially appealing.

Whether a cabin owner prefers summer memorabilia, winter accessories, or a mixture of both, there are plenty of vintage sports related items to choose from to add interest and color to a cabin's décor.

Sailboat and golf trophies were offered for sale in the 1939 Bennett Brothers catalog. These types of trophies can add interesting touches to a cabin's décor.

Vintage sports trophies offer unique accessories to use in decorating a cabin. Personal family trophies from long ago sailboat races, golf tournaments, ski races, or tennis tournaments would be especially appropriate. If none of these are available, older trophies of these types have become collectible and can be found on line or in antique malls. Pictured are three trophies from the 1940s and 1950s awarded for golf and tennis. The trophies are 9.25"-9.5" tall. (1950s golf figure, $25-$35; 1940s tennis figure, $45-55; cup, $20+).

Advertisement for "the new 1926 Champion Evinrude Sport Twin" motor. The Evinrude Motor Co. of Milwaukee, Wisconsin was the first firm to patent an outboard motor in 1911. Framed advertisements of this type could be used, along with old photographs or magazine covers, to decorate a cabin wall. This ad appeared in the *Field and Stream* magazine in December 1926. (Complete magazine, $15).

The famous Chris-Craft Express Cruiser was pictured in this advertisement in the *Field and Stream* magazine in December 1943. The Chris-Craft Corporation in Algonac, Michigan, like most American manufacturing firms, was involved in war production instead of boat production during the years of World War II. Most of the large companies continued to advertise during the war years so they would retain customers at war's end. This ad states that the firm was "World's Largest Builder of Motor Boats." A collection of framed vintage Chris-Craft ads would also make an interesting cabin wall arrangement. (*Field and Stream* magazine, $7.50).

A vintage bathing suit, photograph, and framed magazine cover have been grouped together to make a cabin wall display. An arrangement could also be made using a variety of sports-related magazine covers or a collection of old photographs. The suit and photograph are both circa 1920s and the *Judge* magazine cover titled "Flaming Youth" is dated August 28, 1926. The bathing suit is labeled "U.S. Knitting and Textile Mills/ 100% All Wool/Baltimore, MD." (Bathing suit, $45+; unframed photograph, $15; magazine cover $25+).

When decorating a summer cabin, vintage water skis can be displayed instead of snow skis to add a touch of summer sports to the décor. If the cabin owners have participated in the sport of water skiing for many years, old skis may still be occupying a corner of the garage or boat house. If not, garage sales held near popular lakes would offer a good place to look for the skis, as well as old life jackets and boat cushions which are currently collectible. Vintage swimming caps have also been added to the collectible market. They were made in a variety of colors and styles and many included interesting added decorations. A summer cabin bathroom could be made unique with several unusual caps displayed on pegs or "heads." The water skis are circa early 1960s and are marked "Cascade/Catamoran Pat No. 3059025." The bathing cap is marked "U.S. Royal Water-tite Swim Cap." The circa 1960s bathing suit is marked "I. Magnin Co." The life jacket is also circa 1960s and carries a label which reads Sea King/Buoyant Vest/Stock No. 60-9152 Model AK Adult/Manufactured for Montgomery Ward." (Wood water skis, $45-$55; bathing cap, $14; life preserver, $10; bathing suit, $15-$20).

For a boat lover, a collection of vintage sailboat memorabilia can add a personal touch to a cabin's décor. Pictured are a framed print from the 1930s ($15-$20), a decorated wood souvenir anchor from Moberly, Missouri circa late 1930s ($15), and a heavy metal sailboat ($8-$10). Vintage toy sailboats are also available through the Internet and toy shows.

Other boat related collectibles include a wind-up tin litho motor boat circa 1950s and a picture puzzle which features motor boats at the shore of Grand Lake, Colorado. The puzzle is unique because it was made to be sold as a souvenir in the village of Grand Lake. It is likely that puzzles were also marketed with scenes of other resort areas. The puzzle is marked "TUCO/INTERLOCKING TV SERIES 3950/PICTURE PUZZLE 200 PIECES. MFG BY TUCO WORKSHOPS INC. LOCKPORT, N.Y." The boat is marked in a circle "T. Cohn Inc./Made in USA." It measures 7.5" long. (Boat $45; puzzle, $20).

Below:
During the late 1930s and 1940s sailboats were pictured on a variety of useful products. Included were glasses, pitchers, dinnerware, canister sets, refrigerator dishes, bedspreads, blankets, lamps, bookends, and trays. Pictured are a pair of bookends and a tray. They are both made of imitation wood type material popular in the late 1940s and 1950s. The tray includes a sticker on the back reading "ORNAWOOD." The sailboat bookends also include a worn sticker which looks like it says "SYROCO WOOD/Syracuse, N.Y." Any vintage sailboat decorated merchandise from earlier years would be fun to use in a summer cabin. (Tray, $8; bookends, $20-$25).

Antique framed calendars and vintage magazine covers featuring sporting activities fit together nicely when used to decorate a cabin wall. The most unusual are the examples from the early 1900s which feature female participants. Women, in those days, were not as athletic as those of today so it is surprising that so many women were used as subjects on these products. Pictured is a framed calendar for 1909 entitled "The Golf Girl," which features a woman holding a golf club. The calendar advertisement is for "HENDERSON & PRICE/THE FURNITURE MEN/MARYVILLE, MO."

The cover of the *Sunday Magazine of the Sunday Record-Herald* (Chicago) pictures a woman who appears to be on her way to use her snowshoes for a winter walk in the woods. The magazine is from December 19, 1909, the same year as the calendar. (Unframed calendar, $35+; unframed magazine, $25+).

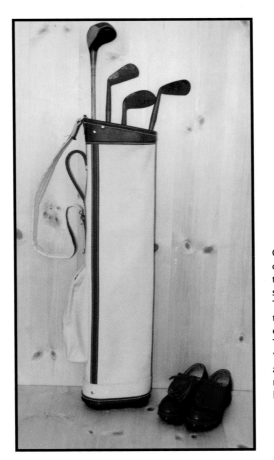

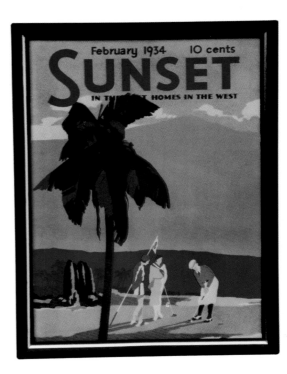

Vintage magazine cover features a threesome (two women and one man) playing a game of golf. It came from the cover of *Sunset* magazine for February 1934. Sports magazine covers, similar to this one, are especially appealing because they can be matted and nicely framed to be used in decorating a cabin. See also the Swimming and Skiing covers for other collectible examples. (*Sunset* golf magazine, $30+).

Older golf bag and clubs, along with a pair of women's golf shoes currently occupy a place of honor in the corner of a summer cabin. This type of bag was made for decades, usually of a twill type material with synthetic leather-looking trim, sometimes referred to as "par-hyde." The mismatched wood handled clubs have been collected to display in the golf bag. The golf shoes are brown leather with flaps on the front of each shoe. (Bag, $50; shoes, $20-$25; clubs, $40-$50 each).

The golf clubs displayed in the bag include a wood marked "KROVDON," an iron marked "Mid Iron/Columbia Special," and another iron labeled "MacGregor Dayton." A wedge club carries the mark of "Dick Nelson" as well as "Professional Golfer Assn. Custom Made." Additional markings are "Sweet Spot" and "......KRO-FLITE."

Old tennis rackets, like skis, can be used to decorate small spaces above or beside doors, or combined with appropriate tennis photographs, magazine covers, souvenir programs, and pennants to cover a large wall space. Like all cabin collectibles, the more personal items that can be incorporated into the arrangement, the more meaningful it will be. Pictured are two early tennis rackets which feature different shapes. The elongated racket is marked only "CROWLEY, MILNER & CO." and the other one carries a decal type marking which reads "Alphe" plus one more indiscernible letter along with "trade mark." The rest of the label reads "School and ...... Products." ($25+ each).

This newer version croquet set probably dates from the 1960s. It includes six mallets, six balls, wickets, two posts, and a stand. These newer sets can add color to a cabin porch. ($25-$40).

Vintage croquet sets can be useful both in the decorating of a cabin and for the entertainment of guests. A variety of different sets could be displayed on an enclosed porch or an old boxed set might be placed on a shelf or used as part of a corner arrangement of tennis rackets or golf clubs. Pictured is an early croquet set in its original box labeled "ECLIPSE CROQUET." The set includes pieces for six players. ($50+).

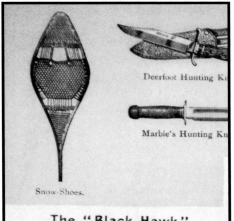

The "Black Hawk" Snow-Shoes.

No. 1. Given for one new subscription and $1.35 extra. Price $2.50.

No. 2. Given for one new subscription and $2.10 extra. Price $3.50.

No. 3. Given for one new subscription and $2.80 extra. Price $4.50. In every case sent by express, charges paid by receiver.

These Shoes have been offered by us for a number of years and have given excellent satisfaction. They are made with a turned-up Canadian toe, good quality rawhide netting, and are closely woven. They are genuine Indian made. We offer three sizes: No. 1, 9 x 28 inches, for children; No. 2, 11½ x 37 inches, for ladies and boys; No. 3, 14 x 42 inches, for men.

In addition to summer sports, winter activities can also add interesting equipment that can be used to decorate a cabin. Vintage snowshoes are very appealing. The early examples, made by Indians, are especially desirable. This advertisement in the *Youth's Companion* for Oct. 21, 1909 featured the "Black Hawk" snowshoes. They came in three sizes: children's, women's, and men's, priced from $2.50 to $4.50 for each pair. The copy reads "they are made with a turned up Canadian toe, good quality rawhide netting and are closely woven. They are genuine Indian made."

This wall arrangement includes two different sizes of large snowshoes. The pair on the bottom is similar to the ones offered in the Sears catalog. The Sears models were 60" long. A set of more recent children's snowshoes, a pair of wood skis, and a cane fishing pole complete the display. Large wall spaces are needed for this type of arrangement. (Longer snowshoes, $175+ each pair, skis, $75+ pair).

A set of wood skis and bamboo poles could add interest to any wall or corner in a cabin. These bamboo poles include wrapped leather handles and are marked "ARWEST SPORT" ($125 pair). The skis are circa late 1930s and were made in Norway ($185). *Courtesy of Avalanche Ranch, Redstone, Colorado.*

133

All kinds of ski accessories can be used in cabin decoration. These include old posters, shoes, hats, sweaters, and signs. Pictured are a pair of wood skis circa late 1940s, buckled square toed ski boots also circa late 1940s, a Vail, Colorado ski poster circa 1960s and a metal ski area telephone sign. (Skis, $100; poster, $25; shoes, $45; sign, $45+).

This vintage suede snapshot album from Sun Valley, Idaho pictures a skier on its front cover. This early ski resort was very popular with people who worked in the motion picture industry in the late 1930s and early 1940s. A movie called *Sun Valley Serenade* was produced by 20th Century Fox in 1941. It starred skating star Sonja Henie. The album could actually be used for its original purpose, filled with skiing photos and placed on a cabin table along with a box of postcards from the area. ($25+).

Older ski sweaters can also add color and interest to the inside of a winter cabin. These are not easy to find as they were made of wool and were usually discarded because of moth holes. The Spiegel Fall and Winter catalog for 1944 pictured a man's sweater that would be appropriate to use for decoration in a ski cabin. It sold for $9.95.

In addition to generic ice skates, many companies promoted their skates by using the names of famous figure skaters or hockey players. These types of skates can be used as a conversation piece as well as a touch of nostalgia when displayed in a winter cabin. Pictured is a framed advertisement from the NESTOR JOHNSON MFG. CO. in Chicago, Ill. circa 1938. The skates are endorsed by three-time Olympic ice skating champion Sonja Henie and Chicago Blackhawk hockey star Johnny Gottselig. Each skate bears one of the stars' names. Also shown is a pair of the Nestor Johnson woman's size six Sonja Henie skates. These skates are marked "Sonja Henie" on the metal plate attached to the bottom of the shoe. The remainder of the original box also came with the skates. Sonja Henie won the women's Olympic gold medal in figure skating in 1928, 1932, and 1936. She later had a successful career in Hollywood starring in ice skating related movies. Men's figure skates were also produced by Endicott Johnson in Endicott, New York capitalizing on the Dick Button name. He was the winner of the men's Olympic gold medal in figure skating in 1948 and 1952. He has continued his association with the skating industry as a television commentator. His picture appears on the front of the box circa 1950s. (Unframed advertisement, $10+; Sonja Henie skates, $20-$25; Dick Button box, $8-$10.)

This rustic coat rack has been used to display several pairs of old ice skates. Included are vintage men's shoe skates which are marked "Star Manufacturing Co. Ltds./Halifax-Canada," women's shoe skates made in Canada, and a pair of boy's shoe skates marked "MCING CANADA Tempered Blade." The pack basket has also been filled with an assortment of ice skates including two pair of wood and steel skates marked with a decal reading "NV STOOMSCH AATSEN???/ Grand Prix/St. Louis U.S.A." and a pair of more easily found metal clamp-on skates with blades marked "HARDEMED." Double runner children's skates are also included. They are circa 1950s and carry a "Globe-Union Inc. Milwaukee WS. U.S.A." marking. They are also incised "Jack-n-Jill." The skates were to be clamped to the child's shoes. (Coat rack, $100+; pack basket, $100+; Star skates, $10+; women's skates, $20; boy's skates with box, $30-$40, wood-steel skates, $40 pair; clamp-on men's skates, $20 with rust; and children's skates, $10).

Any boxed sporting product is always worth displaying in a related cabin arrangement. Pictured is a never used pair of boy's hockey skates in their original box. The box labels reads "Junior Outfit/B-A-S-C-O #0312 size 1." On the bottom of the skates is marked "MCINC CANADA Tempered Blade." ($30-$40).

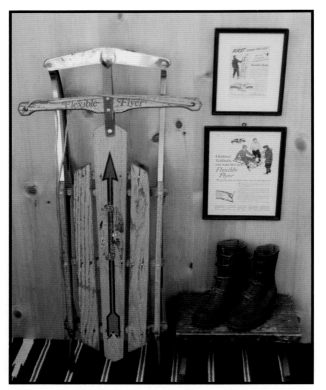

In addition to snowshoes, skis, and ice skates, sleds also provide an interesting decorating tool for cabin owners. Whether they are the large horse drawn variety *(See Exterior Accents chapter)*, a toboggan example, or an ordinary vintage, kids sled, they can be displayed in a variety of ways. The most expensive children's sleds are the early wood ones, circa 1900, similar to the "Rosebud" example from the 1941 Orson Wells *Citizen Kane* movie. They can sell for $1,000 or more. Early "Bob" sleds (long sled with steering "wheel") can also be expensive. Most cabin dwellers settle for European or American made sleds of a more recent vintage. *(See Miscellaneous chapter for photo of a European wood sled).* Sleds can be hung on an outside wall of a cabin or on a sheltered porch. They can be placed beside an outside door *(See Miscellaneous chapter)*, or grouped with other items such as ice skates, old fashioned overshoes, and early framed advertisements. Sleds can also be placed near Christmas trees or fireplaces during the holiday season to be used to hold colorfully wrapped gifts or Santa dolls. Pictured is a vintage Flexible Flyer sled marked on its back "44 x 9A Model/Winter Product/From/FLEXIBLE FLYER/400 Lake Road/Medina, Ohio 44256." Two framed ads for the sleds are also pictured. Both list S.L. Allen and Co. Inc. of Philadelphia as the maker. The lower ad is from *Child Life* magazine for December 1930. This ad states that Admiral Byrd took a Flexible Flyer sled with him on his trip to the North Pole. The advertisement at the top of the photograph appeared in the *Children's Activities* magazine for December 1951. Also pictured are vintage rubber overshoes in a style worn by boys for decades. They could also be displayed with ice skates and/or ski boots under a bench in a cabin entryway. (Sled, $50; unframed ads, $5 to $15 each, overshoes, $15+).

"Sno-ler" push sled circa 1953. These types of sleds were made for decades beginning in the early 1900s. They were used to transport a small child in the snow. Early sleds can sell for $600 or more. The later models had wheel attachments as well as runners. ($200+). *Courtesy of Avalanche Ranch, Redstone, Colorado.*

Flexible Flyer sleds were made for nearly one hundred years. Production was begun in the early 1900s and the last sleds were made in 1996. Older models will be priced from $100-$150, while the more recent vintage sleds will sell for around $50. This ad for the original firm who produced the sleds (S.L. Allen & Co. Inc. of Philadelphia) appeared in the *Youth's Companion* in the Nov. 27, 1919 issue. The sleds were made in seven sizes at that time ranging from 38" to 63" in length.

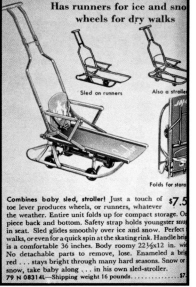

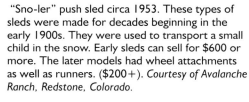

The Sears Christmas catalog for 1953 carried an advertisement for the "Sno-ler" baby sled-stroller for $7.59. The product could be used with either runners or wheels with the "touch of a lever." It folded up for storage.

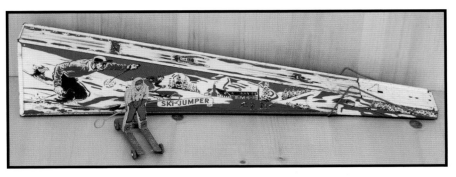

Vintage magazine covers picturing winter sports (not including photographs) are hard to find but well worth the search. When framed, a collection of these covers can provide an exceptional cabin wall arrangement. Shown are three such covers from the 1920s and 1930s. Included are two sledding examples from *Liberty* magazine from January 19, 1935 (Carl Peeufer illustrator), and the *Elks* from February 1924 with a Leslie Thrasher cover. The *Judge* ski design was by Vernon Grant from February 1937. (Unframed complete magazines, *Judge*, $35+; *Liberty*, $10; *Elks*, $15).

Toys always offer a unique touch in any house or cabin. For a winter cabin, ski toys are especially desirable. Several different designs have been made through the years including wind-up skiers, ski ride toys (similar to the roller coaster models), and the pictured Ski-Jumper. It was made by the Wolverine Supply and Mfg. Co. in Pittsburgh, Pennsylvania. This tin lithographed toy works with the help of gravity. The skier on wheels is placed at the top of the jump and rolls down the slope where a "trip" piece sends the figure off the run into a summersault. The toy is 26" long and is circa 1950s. ($100+ with some rust on back of toy).

A collection of dolls in their original ski or ice skating clothing could be displayed on a shelf in groups or combined with vintage framed ads or appropriate magazine covers. Ice skating dolls were produced by many manufacturers for decades so there are lots of models to choose from. Pictured is an 11" tall unmarked composition all original doll with her skis and poles. She is thought to be a Dora Lee doll by Vogue Dolls, Inc., circa late 1930s. Behind her is a *Collier's* magazine featuring a Jon Whitcomb ski cover dated January 14, 1939. (Doll, $300+; unframed magazine, $10+).

Ice skating dolls were made in both composition and hard plastic materials from the 1930s through the 1950s. Many models can still be found in original clothing. Shown is an all composition Nancy Lee doll from the Arranbee Co. circa 1940s. She still has her original tag and box (not pictured). Also shown is a pair of women's ice skates from the 1940s featuring a cuff of imitation fur around the top. The skates are marked "Made in Canada." (Doll, $350+; skates, $20).

Fishing and Hunting Collectibles

Nearly everyone has had a fishing experience during their early years. For some, it was simply the setting for an occasional family outing. For others, it marked the beginning of a lifelong love of fishing and the great outdoors. For owners whose cabins are located near lakes, streams, or rivers, fishing related memorabilia is a must to use in cabin decorating. As in other accessories, those relating to family are the most desirable. These include vintage family fishing photographs, dated fishing licenses, family owned tackle boxes and fishing poles, as well as reels and minnow buckets. Even old boat cushions and fishing hats can be added to a cabin's décor.

Vintage fishing lures have become especially popular in recent years. The first commercial wooden lures were made shortly before 1900. According to Dudley Murphy and Rick Edmisten writing in their book *Fishing Lure Collectibles,* the early companies, which produced these lures, included the Creek Club Bait Co. in Garrett, Indiana, James Heddon and Sons in Dowagiac, Michigan, Pfueger (Enterprise Mfg. Co.) in Akron, Ohio, and the William Shakespeare Co. in Kalamazoo, Michigan. The most collectible and therefore the most expensive lures are those made before 1940. After the end of World War II, most producers began making their lures of plastic. Although wood models are the most desirable, from a distance it is hard to tell the difference.

Lures can be displayed in small wall-hung cabinets, in old barber shop mug holders, or shelves. Specially made coffee tables with an added glass top can also be used. For larger wall shelves or cabinets, a combination of small fishing items including bobbers can be combined to offer a more unique arrangement. A collection of bobbers can also be displayed in a basket or dish on a table top to add color to a cabin interior. An open vintage tackle box may be used to hold a collection of older fishing lures, bobbers, etc. It can be placed on a table or shelf (away from small children and pets). It would be especially appealing if it belonged to a relative.

This porch fishing arrangement includes an old rocking chair, metal tackle box, Falls City minnow bucket, fly rod and reel, fishing hat and boat cushion. The boat cushion measures 15" x 15" x 2" and its label reads "Buoyant Boy/Life Preserver/Manufactured by/Atlas Products Co./St. Paul, Minn." The picture on the front of the cushion depicts two people paddling a canoe. The hat includes a label which reads "DORFMAN/PACIFIC/Oakland, Calif." The fly rod and tackle box are not marked. The Falls City minnow buckets were made by the Metal Ware Division of the Stratton and Terstegge Co. in Louisville, Kentucky. The My Buddy tackle boxes also were produced by the same firm. (Boat cushion, $20; hat, $12; tackle box, $15-$20, minnow bucket, $25+, fly rod and reel, $50).

Wall arrangements can also be made which feature fishing gear or related items. Fishing creels, framed vintage sports magazine covers, calendars which feature fishing pictures, fishing-related neckties, fishing nets, and of course, taxidermy preserved fish can all be combined into interesting wall displays.

Casting reels were invented in the 1870s so fishermen could reach a larger area while fishing. These early reels and poles are also now very collectible. An assortment of poles and other fishing gear can be used to add interest to an entry hall. A rack can be used to hold old poles, while a vintage tackle box, fishing creel, fishing net, fishing hat, and minnow bucket can be displayed on a rustic bench. Vintage fishing boots would also add a unique touch.

Many different sizes and styles of minnow buckets have been produced through the years by a variety of manufacturers. An assortment of these buckets would provide a pleasing arrangement on a cabin porch. They could be displayed on rustic shelves or on a bench. A bucket with an oblong shape makes a unique cabin magazine rack.

Vintage canoes, paddles, boats, motors, cushions, and seats have also recently been added to the collectible list. The most popular seats and cushions are those that are colorful and decorated with designs. If a cabin is large enough, a canoe can be hung from the ceiling for an added touch. Other worn canoes or row boats can be cut in half and used for shelving in a cabin corner. An old row boat could also be filled with potted flowers in the summer and displayed in the yard of a cabin. Vintage paddles are easier to display and are quite attractive. A variety of sizes and colors can be collected and then hung on a cabin or screened porch wall.

An older outboard motor could also be used as part of a porch fishing arrangement. It might be placed in a corner or on a motor stand. Old gasoline cans, oars, fishing poles, boat cushions, and boat seats could be included as part of the display.

Ice fishing also has a following in the colder climates. For those cabin owners who indulge in this kind of entertainment, vintage ice fishing equipment can also be found which can add its own touch when used as an accessory in cabin décor.

Fishing related items are not as plentiful as those shown in the *Wildlife chapter*, but they are useful in cabin decorating and well worth the time and effort to acquire. Vintage plates and old prints featuring fish and fisherman are perfect conversation pieces to use to decorate the walls of a lake house.

Although hunting does not rank as high as fishing in the past experiences of many cabin owners, the display of hunting gear from days gone by can be used to add additional interest to a cabin, especially for hunting enthusiasts. Old hunting outfits, backpacks, and duck decoys are just some of the collectibles from the hunting field that can be used in cabin décor. The clothing can be hung on pegs in an entry hall along with a taxidermy piece *(See Taxidermy and Wildlife Pictorials chapter)* or several sets of antlers in a variety of sizes. A favorite vintage family shotgun or rifle displayed over a fireplace can also add to the hunting lodge look.

Wood duck decoys are popular with collectors. They show well individually or in groups. A large collection can be displayed on wall shelves or one or two of the decoys can be grouped with other items on a fireplace mantle.

Whether a cabin owner is a fishing enthusiast or a hunter, many different items relating to these sports can be used to add interest to both the inside and outside of a cabin. The opportunities are as varied as the decorators' imagination.

A collection of the authors' family fishing licenses and pictures have been mounted and framed to make an interesting "picture" for a summer cabin. The licenses date from 1938 to 1952 and are reminders of fishing trips to Missouri, Oklahoma, Kansas, Minnesota, and Canada. The family fishing photos are also from a variety of trips through the years.

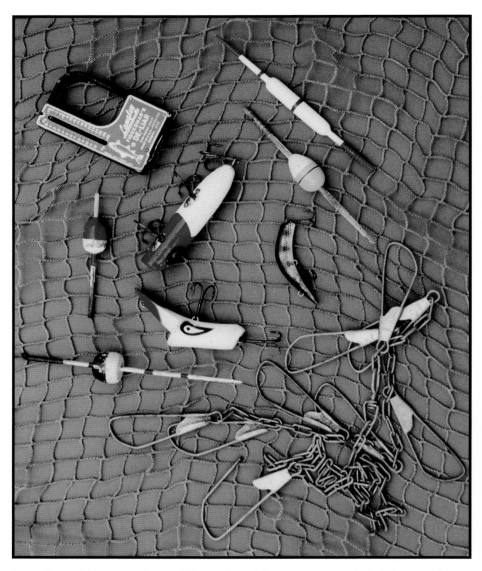

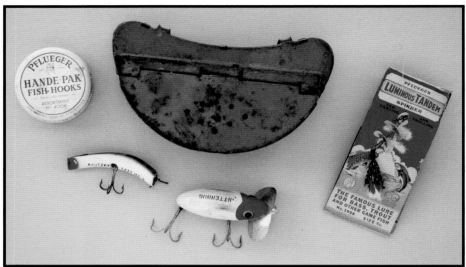

Other vintage fishing items that could be displayed in small wall shelves include an unmarked metal bait box and a Pflueger "Luminous Tandem Spinner for Casting and Trolling." It is still on its original card marked "the Pfluegers/Akron, Ohio" circa late 1950s early 1960s. Also pictured is a metal box of Pflueger fish hooks, a plastic Kautzky Lazy Ike-2 lure as well as a plastic Jitterbug lure. The Jitterbug was made by Fred Arbogast and Co. in Akron, Ohio. (Bait box, $18; lures, $6-$8 each; fish hooks in tin, $3; spinner, $5-$8).

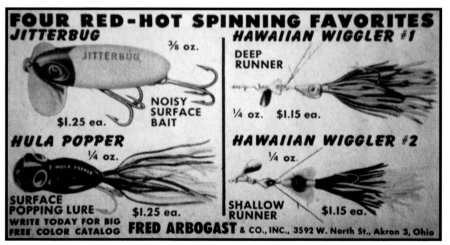

A sampling of fishing items that could be used in a fishing arrangement. Included is an early "Langley Fisherman's DE-LIAR" made by Langley in San Diego, California. This model which weighed fish up to 28 pounds and measured to 42" was featured in the Sears 1955 Christmas catalog at a cost of $2.50. It includes its original box which states "PAT. PEND." ($10). Also pictured are some wood bobbers ($3-$5 each), a metal fish stringer ($8), and three vintage lures. They include a marked "South Bend/BASS-ORENO" wood lure ($18-$20), a vintage plastic Lazy Ike made by the Lazy Ike Corp. in Fort Dodge, Iowa (replaces the minnow according to advertising). It came with its original box bottom ($8), and a wood Kautzky Top Ike ($18-$20).

The Jitterbug plastic lure was advertised in the *Western Sportsman* magazine for Jan.-Feb. 1952. It sold for $1.25. A Hula Popper lure as well as two spinners were also included in the Fred Arbogast ad.

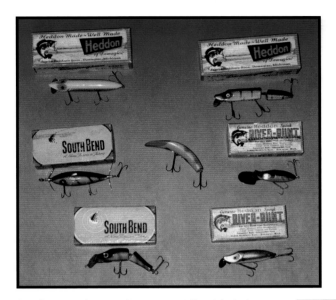

A collection of vintage lures, especially with their original boxes, is hard to find. These lures were all used by one fisherman many years ago. The collection includes four wood lures and three made of plastic. Original prices still visible on two boxes are $1.20 and $1.35. The lures made by James Heddon's sons of Dowagiac, Michigan include the two lures on the top and the two River-Runt models. On the top left is the Vamp-Spook (plastic) and on the right the Jointed Vamp (wood). The River-Runts are both made of plastic and are marked "Heddon/River/Runt/Spook/Floater" (top) and "Heddon/Vamp/Spook" (bottom). The two lures made by the South Bend Bait Co. of South Bend, Indiana are both made of wood. The top South Bend example is a Nip-I-Diddee No. 910 YP. The lower lure is a Pike-Oreno No. 2956. Some of the brochures that came in the boxes were dated from 1946-48. (Wood mint in box lures, $30-$40 each; plastic mint in box lures, $20+ each). *From the collection of Larry Pittman. Photograph by Marilyn Pittman.*

After assembling a collection of lures, bobbers, and other small fishing accessories, they can be mounted in shelves and displayed on a cabin wall. This rustic shelf unit is perfect for this purpose. The items can be mounted with the use of tacks. (Shelf, $10+).

For a larger display unit, old barber shop mug shelves are ideal. This one includes a decoration of antlers on its top. The wood fish hanging on the side are new. Family fishing pictures have also been included in this display. (Antique barber shop shelves, $300-$350).

A basket of bobbers can add a touch of color to a table top in a summer cabin. The wood examples are the most desirable ($3-$5 each; basket, $6-$8).

For a more complete display, a tackle box can be supplemented with other items as shown here. An appropriate *Outdoor Life* magazine cover and fly fishing neck tie have been hung on the wall behind the tackle box. The *Outdoor Life* is dated April, 1943 ($9) and the fly fishing decorated necktie carries its own label. It reads "MATHENY'S/JUNEAU, ALASKA." The tie itself is marked "ALL SILK/individually/Hand Painted/in/California/by/ HOLLYVOGUE." ($20-$25)

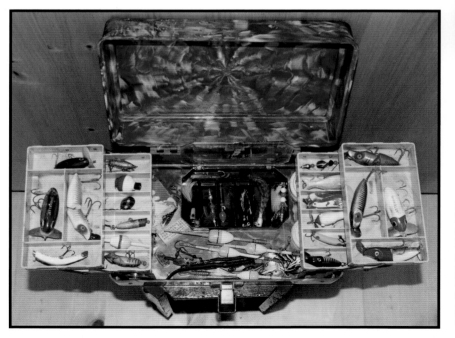

It is unusual to find a vintage-filled tackle box just the way a fisherman left it. For a fortunate collector, this type of box could be displayed on a lower shelf so the inside treasures can be seen. The pictured tackle box belonged to Clyde Shipe from Sunbury, Pennsylvania. Most of the contents are from the 1950s and early 1960s. It includes twelve lures made of plastic and two small ones made of wood. Most of them were produced by Heddon. An assortment of spinners, wood bobbers, fish hooks, and other small items are included. The tackle box itself is made of a heavy plastic and is marked "PLANO MOLDING CO./PETE HEMMING/ PLANO/ ILLINOIS." ($100-$125).

Another fishing related item that can be used in cabin decorating is a vintage calendar. This calendar from 1954 was designed as a promotional item and was sold to local businesses. The calendar text reads "Advertise with the/Grand S Line/365 Days a Year/Good Will Creates Friends." (Calendars, $25-$35 each depending on date, picture, and condition).

Many fisherman have had their "big one" preserved through the use of taxidermy. For the cabin owner who would like to own one of these prize fish from the past, many antique malls as well as the Internet frequently offer them for sale. A fish caught by a family member would make a mounted fish more personal. Pictured is a 3.5 pound rainbow trout pulled from a lake near Rocky Mountain National Park by the co-author's son at the age of ten. The fish is surrounded by a vintage creel ($50), unusual metal stringer ($15-$20), minnow bucket ($25+), and fishing net ($75). Also pictured is a new "gone fishin" sign. (Cost of taxidermy, $200; mounted fish in shop, $100 depending on size and condition).

The back of an open log stairway provides a perfect setting for three vintage fishing creels. *From the collection of Bob Scott.*

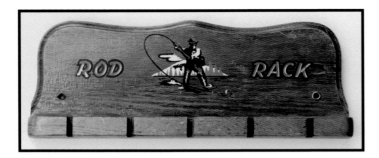

Vintage fishing rods can be displayed on commercially-made wood "Rod Racks." Circa 1950s, these racks have also been seen personalized with the owner's name. (Rack, $20).

A collection of vintage minnow buckets displayed on a bench on a cabin porch. The examples pictured on the bench include buckets labeled "Falls City" (regular and "Wade in" sizes), "J.C. Higgins Minnow Bucket" (carried by Sears), and "Nu-Airflo/ Feeds em Air." Under the bench are "Falls City the Angler's Choice" and "Old Pal Floating Minnow Bucket." (Small Falls City, $25; larger buckets, $25-$35 each.) *Cabin porch courtesy of Glenn and Douglas Land; bench from the collection of Wyatt Sabadosh.*

Since the J.C. Higgins minnow bucket has an oval shape, it can be used to hold magazines. Pictured are vintage hunting and fishing magazines from the 1920s to 1950s. (*Field and Stream*, December 1926, $15-$20; December 1943, $7-$10; *Western Sportsman* 1940s-1950s, $3 each.)

Even a small cabin hallway allows space for a display of fishing collectibles. The contemporary boat has been filled with old fishing lures and bobbers while the pegs below hold a vintage fishing net, minnow bucket, and a new set of wood fish. A well used oak canoe paddle is also pictured.

Other items that could be combined with the boat seat for a porch display include this "6 Evinrude" outbound motor circa 1960s, the weathered oars, and the vintage gasoline can with its original label reading "Quality Heavy Metalware/Deluxe/Schueter Mfg. Co., St. Louis, Mo." (Motor, $125; oars, $50; gasoline can, $15-$20).

Old boat seats like the one pictured can be used in a fishing display on a porch or entryway. This unmarked example is made of metal and wood. A bucket of vintage reels rests in its seat. Included is a large Salmon side winder reel. (Boat seat, $85). *Courtesy Avalanche Ranch, Redstone, Colorado.*

This very old unidentified boat motor is displayed on a vintage boat stand marked "EVINRUDE." These types of stands work well to display motors on a porch or even inside a cabin. *Courtesy of Grand Elk Marina and Beach Club, Granby, Colorado.*

This old metal bucket is filled with winter ice fishing flags called tip-ups. The flags came up when the fisherman got a bite. ($22 each.) *Courtesy Avalanche Ranch, Redstone, Colorado.*

Vintage winter backpack made of animal hide that could have been used on hunting trips. It measures 10.75" wide and 18.75" tall. The label reads "P. DUTOIT/ 1940/Moudon/2." The pack includes an added pocket as well as the large opening at the top. ($150).

Older ice fishing equipment can also be used for interesting accessories in a winter cabin. Since fishermen remain seated close to a hole in the ice, the poles used for ice fishing are much shorter. This example could be displayed with other ice fishing items or hung on a cabin wall along with regular fishing poles. ($60+)

These interesting plates decorated with fish are marked "Porcelain Lo France." They would be very attractive displayed in a cabin dining area either on the wall or in a cabinet. (Not enough examples to determine a price). *Courtesy of Little Bear's Antique Mall, Glenwood Springs, Colorado.*

True Life Wood Decoys

Carefully shaped and seasoned. Natural glass eyes. Natural color. Will not sink. 4 drakes, 2 hens, in half dozens. Shipping weight, ½ dozen, 14 pounds.

6 K 693	Mallard	½ Dozen	
6 K 694	Canvasback	½ Dozen	**$4.45**
6 K 695	Black Duck	½ Dozen	
6 K 696	Bluebill	½ Dozen	

The Sears Fall and Winter catalog for 1935-1936 carried an ad for "true life wood decoys" for $4.45 each. The copy stated that the decoys were "carefully shaped and seasoned" and featured natural glass eyes. The decoys included mallards, canvas back, black duck, and bluebill models.

Wood duck decoys, circa 1930s-40s, thought to be handmade. The one on the top step has glass bead eyes. A collection of these types of decoys can be displayed on a shelf or singly on a fireplace mantle. Duck decoys are very collectible and depending on age and condition can cost up to thousands of dollars. ($75 to $100 each). *From the collection of the Larry Zillner family.*

Old hunting gear can also be used for decorating a cabin whose owner likes to hunt. Wool hunting outfits can be hung on pegs near an entryway or on an enclosed porch. This example includes a label reading "Est. 1880/Woolrich/ WOOLRICH WOOLEN MILLS/ WOOLRICH, PA." Old steel traps are also shown. (Outfit, $50; traps, $10 each).

The Spiegel Fall and Winter catalog for 1944 advertised a similar wool hunting outfit. The coat was priced at $12.95 and the pants cost $7.45. A wool cap was available for $1.15 while a corduroy cap was only 78¢.

A muzzleloader gun, pouch, and powder horn could be hung on a log cabin wall as reminders of the past. This .54 caliber percussion muzzleloader gun was hand made by Estes and its owner occasionally uses it on hunting trips. Vintage family related guns would also be appropriate items to display on a cabin wall. *Gun, pouch and powder horn from the collection of Don Finnicum. Photograph by Marilyn Pittman.*

147

Taxidermy and Wildlife Pictorials

This hunting cabin in Ohio includes a variety of wildlife taxidermy used for decoration in its "Great Room." Included are a deer head, bear skin. and several sizes of antlers. Large snowshoes flank the deer head over the rock fireplace. *From the cabin of Ardith and Don Finnicum. Photograph by Marilyn Pittman.*

Collectibles featuring wildlife fit naturally into a cabin of today. Since tastes vary, owners have a variety of examples to choose from. There are commercially produced items which feature images of deer, elk, antelope, bears, geese, and ducks, and there are the life-size taxidermy mounts that add a different dimension. Bear skins are also available for those who like a Theodore Roosevelt hunting cabin look. In addition, cabin furnishings have been made of animal parts in years past. Lamps made of deer or elk hooves, carving sets made of antlers, light fixtures with antler accents, and even wreaths made from pheasant feathers or antlers can add interest to a cabin's décor.

Artwork that shows the animals in their natural setting is preferred by many collectors. Deer and elk images have always captured the attention of artists and this was especially true in the early part of the twentieth century. Many representations of their work can be found in prints and on plates produced during this period.

Plates made by Buffalo Pottery in its wildlife series are especially desirable. Buffalo Pottery (New York) produced sets in the early part of the twentieth century, which featured deer, fish, or fowl as decorations. The deer sets are especially appealing for cabin owners. The complete set included a platter and six plates. According to authors Violet and Seymour Altman writing in *The Book of Buffalo Pottery,* all of the designs were based on paintings created by R.K. Beck, a well-known wildlife painter. These were applied to the plates and platters by decal. Many of the plates and platters include the painter's name. The Altman's list the wildlife sets as follows: white-tailed deer platter, plus plates featuring moose, eastern white-tailed deer, elk, sika deer, fallow deer, and caribou deer. Both a male and a female were pictured on each of the plates and platter. The Larkin Company used several of the sets as premiums from 1908-1914.

Many other plates featuring deer or elk were produced in Bavaria-Germany. A collection of these plates can be grouped together on a wall, plate rack, or fireplace mantle to remind owners and visitors alike of the original inhabitants of the area surrounding a cabin.

Many cabins are located where deer, elk, and the occasional moose still come calling to eat the shrubs, flowers, or grass in the area. The coexistence of man and nature enables cabin owners to enjoy spectacular views of wildlife from their porches and windows, while being tolerant of the damage to their manicured landscapes. Bears, also, are plentiful in many cabin environments. They have been known to break into cabins or houses in their hunt for food.

Lovely old deer and elk framed prints, circa early 1900s, can be used to hang on cabin walls but they are getting harder to find. More plentiful are the printed velvet "tapestry" wall hangings, which feature deer and elk images. Most of these included fringe on both ends of the fabric. The condition of the fringe should give the buyer an indication as to whether the piece is an old one or a more recent product. Also readily available are the 1950s and 1960s "Paint by

Number" paintings. For cabin owners who like a little humor in their décor, these are very appealing. The Smithsonian honored the phenomenon with a 50th anniversary exhibit a few years ago. The paint sets were still available at that time but, of course, not as popular as when they were first marketed.

In addition to plates and prints, plaques featuring several different deer and elk head designs were used to decorate homes in the 1940s and 1950s. Many of these pieces were made by the "Ornamental Arts & Crafts" firm.

The most expensive wildlife representations are the antique "German Black Forest" hand-carved pieces. Although these types of decorations were made for many years, the early ones, circa late 1800s and early 1900s, are the most desirable.

Many other vintage objects featuring wildlife images had a practical purpose. These included pin trays, pitchers, ashtrays, decorated boxes, tie holders, pipe holders, television lamps, and trays. Any of these items can add an interesting decorating touch to a cabin's décor.

Puzzles were also produced which feature pictures of deer, elk and bears. After an older puzzle is assembled, it could be placed under glass on a coffee or lamp table to add an unusual touch of color.

For cabin owners who are also hunters, cabin walls offer perfect backgrounds to display deer, elk, or antelope trophies. These mounts display especially well over a fireplace mantel or in log homes with cathedral-type ceilings. Vintage mounts can be purchased in antique shops or malls, at flea markets, or on the Internet to provide the look of a hunting cabin.

Whether a cabin decorator prefers prints or plates depicting deer and elk or deer and elk mounts hanging on the walls, no cabin décor would be complete without some attention being paid to the animals that inhabit the territory in the surrounding area.

No cabin would be complete without some space dedicated to wildlife replicas. Very rare, circa 1870s, German Black Forest hand-carved walnut owl. The 9" tall owl has glass eyes and wings which are carved slightly away from the body. The head lifts to allow small items to be placed inside. The bear is also a vintage German Black Forest product featuring especially nice carving. He is made of lindel wood. Many different designs of Black Forest wildlife figures were produced covering a period of many years. Although the rarer examples aren't readily available, less rare or more recent Black Forest wood carvings can be found. Displayed in a glass case or assembled on a fireplace mantle, these wildlife replicas would add a special touch to a cabin's décor. (Owl, $2,700; bear, $1,200). *Courtesy of Little Bear's Antique Mall, Glenwood Springs, Colorado.*

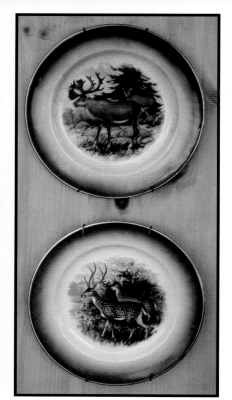

Other vintage china items were also produced which featured wildlife decoration. An example is this "pin tray" which could be used for its original purpose or hung on the wall. It is marked "Three Crown ..../Germany 224." A drawing of three crowns also is part of the marking. ($45+).

Antique plates featuring images of deer, elk, or other wildlife can be hung on cabin walls, placed in plate racks or displayed in vintage cabinets to add interest to a cabin kitchen or dining area. Some of the most collectible of these types of plates are those made by Buffalo Pottery located in Buffalo, New York. The firm did a series of plates and platters which pictured several different designs of wildlife. Two of the six deer plates are shown here. The top plate pictures the caribou and the sika deer are on the bottom plate. ($35-$45 each).

The Buffalo Pottery deer series also included platters. White-tailed deer decorate this platter. It is marked "BUFFALO POTTERY." A buffalo figure is also included as part of the Buffalo Pottery mark. The platter is 15" wide. The name of the creator of the original painting, "R.K. Beck," also appears at the bottom of the design. The large plate on the top carries no mark and is not a Buffalo Pottery product. It pictures two deer. (Platter, $75+; plate, $40+).

Another Buffalo Pottery plate in the deer series pictures two elk. Each plate pictures both a male and female of the species shown. All of the Buffalo Pottery plates appear to be marked "BUFFALO POTTERY." The unknown elk plate shown in the top part of the picture is unmarked. (Buffalo Pottery plate, $35-$45; unmarked, $20-$25).

Vintage pictures of deer, elk, or other wildlife, circa early 1900s, are especially appealing to use for decorating cabin walls. Reproductions of the old prints are readily available but the antique ones require more effort for a collector to locate, especially in their original frames. This wall arrangement features three deer in a vintage framed print titled "A Noble Family." In addition, antlers and an old oak wall telephone are also included. The mouthpiece of the double box phone is marked "THE STROMBERG CARLSON TEL. MFG. CO. PAT. DATE Sep. 8 '96" (1896). (Picture, $75; antlers, $35+; phone, $400).

Antique elk print with its original frame. The print is titled "The Combat." ($100+).

A vintage framed deer print, a pennant, a black candlestick telephone, and an early mission oak telephone stand can add a feeling of nostalgia to a cabin of today. The print is circa 1910 and the pennant which also features a deer is circa 1940s. It is from "White Mountains/New Hampshire." The telephone stand and bench are circa 1920s. An old 1940s telephone book rests in the open shelf in the stand. The telephone includes an oak ringer box which is not pictured. The phone is marked "Kellogg" on the front and includes the following patent information on the back. "Pat'd-Nov. 26 1901-March 19 1907-April 14 1908." For practical use, a current working phone could replace the antique phone shown in the photograph. (Print, $75+; pennant, $20; telephone, $150+; stand and bench, $200).

151

This large elk picture is made of a very heavy plaster-like material. Similar craftwork was popular in the 1950s. The plaster was poured into a mold, allowed to harden, removed, and painted. This elk example is much larger than most of these plaques. It measures 29.5" wide x 17.5" high. ($75+).

Paint by Number sets have also been designed which feature wildlife. These two examples of deer in their natural habitat have been nicely painted and framed. Many collectors like the "Paint by Number" pictures, apparently because it reminds them of a more innocent time. Although these kinds of pictures aren't for everyone, they do offer an alternative to the elusive antique deer and elk prints. ($20-$25 each).

Printed velvet tapestry wall decoration featuring two elk. Missing or worn fringe indicates the piece is old. Newer examples are also available. ($20-$25).

This pair of plaques featuring a deer and a ram appear to be a little older than 1949 examples featured in the Sears Christmas catalog. Their background is made of a heavy composition-plaster material. Both are marked "Copr Ornamental Arts and Crafts." A variety of these types of plaques were made by this manufacturer and an assortment could be collected to decorate a small vertical wall space beside a closet or door. ($15-$20 each).

Another pair of deer plaques, circa 1950s, also marked "Copr Ornamental Arts and Crafts." *See Miscellaneous chapter* for an ashtray example made by the firm. ($15-$20 each)

Other hobbyists have represented deer and elk images on copper backgrounds using a copper tooled sheet method. These types of pictures are fairly common and groups of them could be assembled to decorate a cabin hall or bathroom wall. ($15+).

The 1947 Sears Christmas catalog carried an advertisement for a "cigarette box and ashtray of walnut-finish pressed wood with duck motif." A removable glass ashtray liner was also included. It sold for 89¢. Pictured is a similar item which features a bear on the lid of the cigarette box. An Indian in a canoe, pinecones, flying ducks, and an elk complete the wide variety of decorations on the item. The glass ashtray is missing. Many products were made of this "pressed wood" during the late 1940s and 1950s, and most of them can be used in the decoration of a cabin. Pinecones, Indian motifs, sailboats, ducks, and covered wagons were just some of the appropriate designs used by a variety of firms to decorate these pieces. ($18-$20).

Picture puzzles can still be purchased dating back to the 1920s. For a collector who is diligent, puzzles can be found which feature cabin related scenes. A collection of these boxed puzzles could be displayed on a shelf or a particularly fine example could be assembled, glued to cardboard, framed, and hung on a cabin wall. Shown is "The Elk," a "Big Star Picture Puzzle" circa 1930s. This puzzle includes 250 pieces and produces a 10" x 14" picture. Other markings on the box are "#1010 Made in U.S.A./Russell/1900/St. Paul." (Puzzle, $30).

Several of the men's hunting and fishing magazines offered duck prints for sale for many decades. Many of these types of prints can be found in antique malls or flea markets. After the prints are matted and framed, they can be used in groups to decorate a cabin wall or combined with other treasures like the pictured ceramic duck television lamp, from 1960. The still-working lamp is marked "MADDOX OF CALIF/Made in USA copyright 60." (Unframed prints $10+ each; lamp, $40-$50).

Mallard duck pipe holder with pipe. During the popular smoking years of the 1930s, 1940s, and 1950s, many accessories were produced to tie-in to this habit. Ashtrays, cigarette boxes, and pipe holders were all made in many different materials and designs which featured horses, ducks, or other wildlife decorations. This duck pipe holder is one of the more unusual examples. It could be displayed on a lamp table, perhaps with a vintage family pipe or humidor. (Holder, $45+; pipe, $10-$12). *Courtesy Little Bear's Antique Mall, Glenwood Springs, Colorado.*

Cabin decorations which feature ducks are very appropriate, especially for those cabins which are near water. Plaques of flying ducks were popular in the 1940s and 1950s and can still be easily found today. The older examples are the ducks made of a chalk-like material. The newer ceramic examples have a shiny surface. Pictured with the ducks is an amateur painting which also features a duck in flight. (Picture, $20+; ducks, $15+ each).

For the cabin owners who are not hunters, old taxidermy pieces can be easily found in antique shops or malls. Many of the early Adirondack camps featured such decorations on their walls and the trend continues to this day. Deer, antelope, elk, and bear trophies are the most popular. Pictured is a large vintage deer head purchased from an antique shop in Arkansas. An older taxidermy piece may include hair loss as well as other problems, so the potential buyer should examine the item carefully. ($175+).

Along with T.V. lamps, television metal trays were also popular during the 1950s. In the late 1940s, before the metal trays caught on with the public, "Hasko" trays were being featured in magazines and catalogs. The trays, as well as matching tumblers, were advertised in the *House Beautiful* magazine in October 1948. The Sears Christmas catalog for 1949 also featured the trays priced at $1.98 for a set of four. The Sears copy stated the trays "were made of molded plywood that has been covered with paper treated to resemble wood grains." The trays were produced by the Haskelite Manufacturing Corp. in Chicago. While several designs were made, the flying ducks would be most appropriate for cabin use. The trays measure 16.75" wide x 7.75" deep. They are marked with HASKO as well as their manufacturer on the back. (Set of four, $10-$15).

This vintage antelope head was sold at an antique mall and aside from some shedding hair, it appears to be in good condition. ($100+).

Bear skins can be hung on walls, used as rugs, or as a throw on a couch or bed. They are also popular with cabin owners, especially for those who live in a cold climate. Pictured is a vintage black bear skin rug purchased at an antique store several years ago. The head is detachable. ($850-$1,000). An old wool comfort hangs on the cabin wall and a mission oak rocker can be seen in the corner.

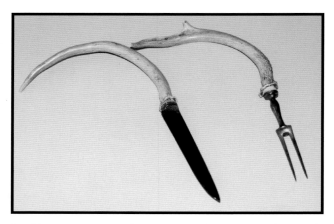

In addition to mounts, other antique and vintage wildlife related items can be acquired to add an old camp-like look to a cabin. Pictured is an antique carving set from the 1800s that includes handles made of antlers. They could be placed in a glass covered case and displayed on a table top or on a kitchen wall. ($295 set). *Courtesy of Little Bear's Antique Mall, Glenwood Springs, Colorado.*

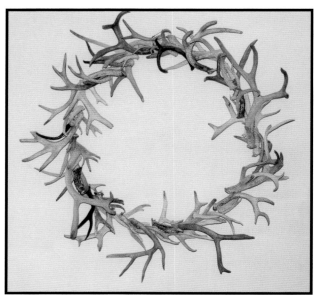

The use of antlers (mostly sheds) to make products for cabin use is still popular. Light fixtures, lamps, and wreaths are some of the most interesting of these items. Pictured is a wreath measuring 46" in diameter. These wreaths can be used as wall decorations or hung over fireplace mantles. ($850+).

This antique piece could be used for either a hat rack or a gun rack. It is decorated with both hooves and antlers as well as a small mirror. The piece was made from walnut and still carries its original label reading "LEEDY'S/TAXIDERMY/DEER SKIN GLOVES/AND JACKETS/NOVELTIES/Munsfield, Ohio."

In addition, wreaths can also be made of other items for use in cabin décor. Included are pinecones, dried flowers, twigs, or feathers. This wreath has been constructed of pheasant feathers. It could be hung on a cabin door, if it is protected from the weather, or displayed on a wall. ($40-$50).

Although most antler light fixtures are quite large, this recent example is small enough to be used in nearly any sized cabin room. It is currently displayed in a cabin kitchen over an antique kitchen table and chairs. ($700+). *From the collection of Bob Scott.*

Vintage Camping and Picnicking Equipment

Many of today's cabin owners were introduced to the countryside during camping and picnicking trips, a fixture of the family vacation during the 1950s and 1960s. The traveling spirit that is so prevalent, even today, may trace back to a desire to imitate our ancestors' treks across the country in their covered wagons as they traveled West to begin new lives.

The National Parks that were begun in the Western part of the United States during the last part of the nineteenth century and the early twentieth century also contributed to this wanderlust. At first, the parks were accessible mostly by train, but as the automobile became more popular, entire families piled into their Ford Model T's to explore the countryside. The cheapest method for traveling was to camp along the way. Tents were produced that could be attached to the outside of a car or a special cot could be purchased that set-up inside the car.

Some early resorts even rented tents to be used by guests. Postcards and photographs of those early camping experiences add historical interest to a cabin of today. The items can be displayed under glass, in a basket, or assembled in an old leather photo album and left on a table for browsing.

By the 1930s, government campgrounds had been established for public use, in which basic necessities were provided. They included picnic tables and campfire rings, plus access to drinking water and restroom facilities. In the mid-1930s, umbrella tents and wall tents were featured in the mail-order catalogs and these types of tents remained in style for decades.

A picnic jug, thermos bottles, and picnic baskets are displayed on a shelf, table, and chair that could be placed on an enclosed porch. These types of jugs and thermos bottles could be used to build a collection or utilized as an accent piece to complement an interesting picnic basket. The rustic shelf and lamp table are new and the chair is an old one made by Old Hickory Furniture Co. The "Tartan Jug" was manufactured by Poloron Products of New Rochelle, New York. The red topped container is labeled "Thermos" and the taller one carries the mark of "Keapsil." The picnic baskets, including the metal one on the table, are unmarked. (Thermos bottles, $7+ each; jug, $20+; metal picnic basket, $20-$25).

The folding wood camp cots (based on the military cots) were also staples of camping trips for many years. Folding wood and canvas chairs and stools also offered simple furnishings for relaxing once the fishing and hiking outings were completed. These chairs can still be used to decorate a deck or yard. *(See Exterior Accents chapter.)*

Camping, then as now, required lighting devices. Most campers packed a flashlight and a gasoline lantern to meet these needs. An "Eveready" flashlight advertisement from 1915 offered a wide supply of lighting styles to choose from. One of these was shaped like a candle in a holder. The Montgomery Ward catalog circa 1916 pictured eight different lanterns that could be used for farm chores or camping. Prices began at 75¢. An interesting collection of old lanterns or vintage flashlights could be easily assembled to add a decorative touch to a cabin. The lanterns can be hung on the inside or outside of a cabin or outbuilding, while flashlights and early battery lanterns can be displayed on wall shelves or in an old cabinet.

Old magazines or books can be found which feature camping scenes on their covers. Old prints, mostly for calendar use, were also produced showing camping scenes from earlier times. In an integrated display combining a wall and a shelf or table top for backgrounds, these types of collectibles can add color and interest to a small area of a cabin.

In the late 1950s and 1960s, many camping enthusiasts upgraded their equipment and invested in a pop-up or travel trailer to increase their comfort. Following this new interest, toy manufacturers began producing the trailers in miniature. These toys can also offer an interesting collection for a cabin owner. They could be combined with toy boats from the past or added to a collection of appropriate childhood family toys to give a more personal touch.

Perhaps no other company has profited more from the interest in camping than the Coleman Company of Wichita, Kansas. One of their recent ads boasts, "And for a hundred years, they've been a beacon in the ultimate test of endurance – the family vacation." In their early years, the firm produced table lamps and light fixtures as well as lanterns. *(See Miscellaneous chapter.)* The early Coleman lanterns were based on a patent purchased from W.H. Hoffstot who had been making the product under the "Sunshine Lamp" name. The Coleman example was being advertised in the Montgomery Ward catalog circa 1916. Products were added over the years to include camp stoves, coolers, camp

tables and chairs, lantern carrying cases, cook kits, and gallon jugs. What is surprising is that all of these products are now very collectible. Many of the Coleman lanterns include the manufacturing date on the bottom of the base, which helps collectors in identifying the older products. A closed-in cabin porch can provide an appropriate place to display a collection of this kind. Since the prices continue to escalate, the display area should be weather proof to protect the investment.

Vintage items produced for picnic use can also add to cabin décor. Picnic baskets, especially, are both useful and attractive. A variety of baskets could be stacked on a kitchen counter and used to hold cookbooks, tablecloths, or other kitchen items. These baskets can also be attractive when placed between the top of the kitchen cabinet and the ceiling, if space is available, and used to store seldom-used kitchen gadgets. Baskets can be found in all sizes and styles. Various materials, such as fiber, wicker, hickory, oak, willow, and even metal have been used to produce picnic baskets, so there are lots of examples to choose from.

Loom woven fiber Redmon picnic baskets can still be found dating from the 1960s and 1970s which still contain the original fittings. Included were stainless forks and spoons, along with plastic plates and mugs. Usually the outfit included a setting for six. The handles on these baskets were metal. Given their durability, most of these baskets can still be put into use for today's picnic outings.

In addition to baskets, vintage picnic jugs and water coolers can make interesting cabin collectibles. The early ones that feature "earthenware" liners are especially desirable. These can be displayed as a collection on a shelf or to accompany a unique picnic basket like the "Hawkeye" from Burlington, Iowa. Enclosed porches offer nice display areas for these items, too. Vintage coolers could be combined with the jugs to add interest. Any of these products, when found in excellent condition, can also be used for their original purpose – a picnic.

Other early picnic items sought out by collectors include enamelware dishes, old silverware, vintage glass jars, and ice cream freezers. *(See Exterior Accents chapter.)*

Whether camping and picnic collections are used as decorations or are put into service during camping or picnic expeditions, these collectibles always bring back memories of past vacations shared with family and friends.

Early camping postcard circa 1910. This must have been a commercial camp since several of these large tents are shown in the background. The family is seated on regular chairs around a table complete with tablecloth. Several glass jars of food are visible as well as a coffee pot to the left. ($8-$10).

A later campsite, in the Adirondack Mountains at Caroga Lake, pictures tents, picnic tables, garbage cans, and stone fireplaces for public use. It was maintained by the government. The vintage car was evidently used to transport the campers to the area. The postcard, circa 1930s, is marked "C.W. Hughes & Co., Inc., Mechanicville, N.Y." Old postcards and vintage photographs *(See Paper Collectibles...chapter)* of early camping experiences are fun to include in a cabin of today. They can be displayed under glass, in a basket, or assembled in an old photo album and left on a table for browsing. ($8-$10).

"Camp Scene in the Adirondacks, N.Y." Printed by the Leighton and Valentine Co., N.Y. City. This appears to be a men's commercial camp, probably used as part of a fishing trip since several canoes and boats are prominently featured in the photograph. ($8-$10).

Ideal Auto Tent

Special Sale Price

Begin now to plan your vacation trip and save money by doing so. A good Touring Tent always is a sound investment. It can be put away until you need it—takes little storage space, and it is as good as new when touring time comes. There are only a few of these tents available at this special low price and it is a certainty that touring tents of this quality will not be priced so low again during this season.

This tent has all the desired features of a touring tent. Made of khaki waterproofed duck. Size, 7 by 9 feet, with 2½-foot back wall. Sewed-in floor cloth and wall next the car makes the tent practically insect proof. Wide band of duck about 29 inches wide goes over the top of the car. Two bobbinett screened windows with cover curtains operated by draw strings. Tent folds into a space of 12 by 24 inches. Shipping weight, 25 pounds.

$16⁸⁵

Reduced from $19.95

60 N 17 .... $16.85

A small Montgomery Ward catalog (No. 6 early 1920s) advertised an "Ideal Auto Tent" 7' x 9' with a 2.5' back wall. It included a floor cloth and wall next to the car. The tent also featured two screened windows. It was priced at $16.85.

Special furnishings were also sold to be used in the tents. Pictured is a very unusual early folding cot that is made of canvas and heavy metal, perhaps iron. Many of the early campers and rustic cabin owners took advantage of army surplus to purchase items that could be useful. Khaki wool Army blankets as pictured were particularly popular. Also shown is an interesting World War I folding canvas bucket. These types of collectibles could be displayed on a protected screened-in porch and called into service to sleep extra guests when necessary. (Blanket, $25; cot, $40; bucket, $40-$50).

New Auto Bed for Tourists

$6⁹⁸ Postpaid

AS CAR BED

Can Be Used With Comfort in Car or Home

This is without doubt one of the most practical auto beds on the market. One-piece construction that is easily set up. Fits any sedan, coach or touring car and positively will not mar the interior. Can be set up outside and easily inserted in car. Can also be used in a home or tent while camping. Frame is made of selected hardwood, walnut stained, reinforced with painted metal fittings. Covered with a heavy 12-ounce khaki color duck. Has no center rail. Heavy adjustable, non-stretch reinforcement extends through the center to insure proper tension at all times. This also prevents occupants from rolling together in the center. The new elevated head end makes this bed more popular than ever. When open, 38 inches wide and 72 inches long; when folded, 6x7x40 inches.

6FC5403¼—Not Prepaid. $6.98
Shpg. wt. 25 lbs.

The Sears Fall and Winter catalog of 1931-1932 pictured a "New Auto Bed for Tourists" for $6.98. The folding bed was designed with one-piece construction for easy assembly.

More useful in today's cabins are the wood and canvas folding deck chairs and stools that were manufactured for decades. When found in good condition, their bright colors can add interest to the patio, deck, or yard of a cabin of today. (Deck chair, $20-$25; stool, $10+). (See also Exterior Accents chapter.)

160

Old flashlights are displayed in an oak rack probably once used for napkins. The tallest flashlight is also the oldest. The bottom is marked "YALE/USE MONO-CELL NO102/YALE ELECTRIC CORP/BROOKLYN, N.Y." The lens is curved and the silver parts appear to be made of brass. The smaller black flashlight is marked "HIPCO/DURO-LITE PATENTS PENDING/MADE IN U.S.A." The metal parts of this flashlight also appear to be made of brass. The metal flashlight with the pointed bottom is marked "RAY-O-VAC" along with a patent number and "MADE IN USA." This flashlight is copper where the silver has worn away ($10-$20 each). The other two silver flashlights are unmarked. A small display like this one can be combined with other camping or picnic items to add interest to a cabin enclosed porch or mud room.

Flashlights of various designs and from many manufacturers have always been important camping accessories. This "Eveready Flashlight" advertisement appeared in the *Women's Home Companion* in December 1915. The flashlights were manufactured by American Ever Ready Works in Long Island City, New York. Their products included pen lights, pocket flashlights, and lantern lights as well as more common models.

The most popular camping lanterns, through the years, have been the gasoline lanterns pictured here in the Sears 1931-1932 Fall and Winter catalog. Although no company is listed as the maker, it looks very much like a Coleman Company product. The lantern sold for $5.98. The illustrations picture the lantern being used to illuminate a tire changing, camping, boating (on the dock), and milking activities.

Lanterns have always played an important role in camp outs whether in the wilderness or in the back yard. These same lanterns were also used by early farmers in their barns as they performed chores. A Montgomery Ward catalog circa 1916 pictured several different styles of these lanterns. *(See Exterior Accents chapter for examples)*. The cheapest lantern sold for only 75¢. A collection of the different styles of lanterns can be hung on porch, exterior, or inside walls of a cabin to offer a touch of nostalgia.

161

Old magazine covers and vintage prints showing camping activities can also add interest to a cabin's décor. This *Ladies Home Journal* cover was painted by Harrison Fisher and is from August 1912. It pictures young women (perhaps Campfire Girls) as they paddle a canoe, take photographs, and relax in a hammock. The covers of the "Campfire Girls" books shown below also feature camping scenes and can be combined with old prints or stacked on a table to add an old look to a current cabin. The books include: *Campfire Girls Lake Camp* by Irene Elliott Benson, copyright 1918 by M. A. Donohue and Co.; *Camp-Fire Girls in the Alleghany Mountains* by Stella M. Francis, copyright 1918 by M.A. Donohue and Co.; and *Campfire Girls in the Maine Woods* by Hildegard G. Frey, copyright by A.L. Burt Company, circa 1915. (Books, $10-$15 each; magazine cover, unframed, $30-$35).

Appropriate vintage toys can also offer interesting collectibles for a cabin owner. This toy station wagon and attached travel trailer date from the 1960s and was a favorite in the authors' family. The car is 11" long and is marked "RAMBLER SIGN OF QUALITY/MADE IN JAPAN." The trailer and hitch also measure 11" long. The two doors on the trailer open. A plastic boat and trailer was originally part of the set. Its popularity stemmed from its similarity to the family's real travel trailer shown in the photograph. Family toys can be augmented with other toys to make a larger collection. Boats, campers, and other trailers could be added to make a unique display. Most of these types of products were produced during the 1960s and 1970s. ($50-$75).

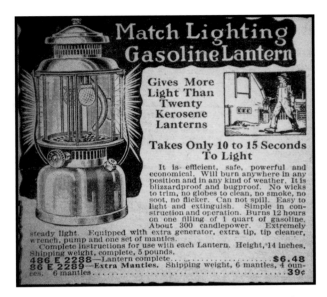

The Montgomery Ward catalog circa 1916 carried an ad for a gasoline lantern which sold for $6.48. It appears to be an early Coleman model made from the Sunshine patent. The copy stated that the lantern gave more light than 20 kerosene lanterns.

Today's collectors are especially fond of all the camping related products manufactured by the Coleman Company of Wichita, Kansas. One of Coleman's early gasoline lanterns is pictured at the left along with a "Sunshine" lantern shown on the right. The Sunshine lantern was invented and patented by W.H. Hoffstot. It was so successful that the Coleman firm purchased his patent and began producing lanterns nearly identical to the Hoffstot model. The Coleman product had a ring on the top and different designs on the metal pieces but otherwise the lamps are the same. The Sunshine lamp is unmarked while the Coleman product is marked "The Air-O-Lantern/Model GL/MFG. Coleman Lamp Co./Wichita, Kans." (Not enough examples to determine a price.) *Courtesy of the Grand Lake Area Historical Society.*

This advertisement from the Butler Brothers Fall and Winter catalog from 1936 offers an assortment of "Coleman Lighting Goods." Included are Coleman table lamps, lanterns, mantles, and generators. The firm produced several sizes of the lamps. The earlier ones had much bigger bases. Overhead lights were also an earlier product manufactured by the firm. *(See Miscellaneous chapter.)* Two different table lamps are pictured. The one priced for $4.15 was made to use gasoline while the $4.50 model used kerosene for fuel. The lanterns used gasoline for fuel except for the one on the right which burned kerosene.

Coleman Company advertisement from 1955. Pictured products include a folding camp stove, stand, carrying case, camp table, flood light lantern, and Coleman portable metal cooler.

Two Coleman lanterns circa 1950s. Both originally carried the same red and white Coleman label on the front. The older model on the right carries no marking on the bottom. It features two mantles and a larger canopy. The metal piece is missing above the base. Its globe is marked "Coleman." The two-mantle lantern on the left is marked "11 55" on the bottom of its base, apparently meaning it was made in 1955. The globe is marked "COLEMAN/PYREX." (1955 lantern, $25-$30; other; $15-$20).

One of the most collectible of the Coleman lanterns is the red model produced in the 1960s and early 1970s. Because most of the lanterns are green, the red ones are harder to find. This model carries only one mantle. The label on the front reads "Coleman Patents Pending." The bottom of the base is marked "The Sunshine of the Night/The Coleman Co. Inc./Wichita, Kansas U.S.A./Model 200A 70." The globe is marked "Pyrex/Made in U.S.A/For/Coleman." The 70 on the bottom indicates the year the lantern was produced. Pictured with the lantern is a carrying case. These cases were also made in red. It carries the red and white "Coleman" label. (Lantern, $25-$30; case, $20-$25).

Coleman lantern from 1968 along with its original box. It is a two-mantle model with a large canopy. It carries the familiar Coleman red and white label on the front and the following information on the bottom: "Coleman/TRADEMARK REGD./ THE SUNSHINE OF THE NIGHT/THE COLEMAN CO. INC./ WICHITA KANSAS U.S.A./10 Model 220F 228F 68". ($20-$25).

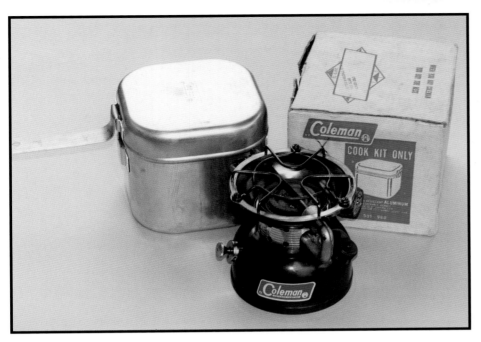

Near mint Coleman cook kit in its original box from 1965. It includes a small stove (the bottom about the size of a lantern base), a pan with a lid and a removable handle. The lid could be used for a frying pan. The stove and handle both fit inside the pan. The lid is marked "Coleman" and the bottom of the pan reads "MFG. IN U.S.A./THE COLEMAN CO. INC./WICHITA, KANS." The stove carries the "Coleman" label as well as "502" on the metal above the base. The bottom of the base is marked "Coleman/TRADEMARK REGD./THE SUNSHINE OF THE NIGHT/THE COLEMAN CO. INC./WICHITA, KANSAS U.S.A./6 Model 502 65." Probably not many of these sets survived in excellent condition as the pan would blacken with use. ($75+).

Vintage picnic accessories also are fun to use in decorating a cabin. Of course, like many camping accessories, these products can also be used for their original purposes. Pictured is a picnic setting as it might have looked many years ago. The picnic table has been set with a vintage red and white tablecloth, ($20+), black and white enamel dishes, old silverware, Ball glass jars to hold the food, a Hawkeye picnic basket, and a jug made by Aladdin Industries. *Picnic table courtesy of Wyatt Sabadosh.*

Left:
Coleman ice chest (made in 1966) and jug with spout. The cooler carries the familiar Coleman label. The body of the chest is metal as is the lid while the inside and bottom are plastic. The handles lock at the top. The top lifts off to reveal a plastic half tray. A spout is located on the lower side to remove water. The bottom is marked "6 66/MADE BY THE COLEMAN CO. INC./WICHITA KANS./USA." The jug's Coleman label also includes "Patents Pending." The handle and the top part of the jug are metal while the bottom spout and lid are plastic. The bottom is marked "6 2 11/MADE BY THE/COLEMAN CO. INC./WICHITA KANS./USA." (Cooler, $40-$45; jug, $35).

Vintage enamel dishes can be fun cabin collectibles either to use for outdoor meals or to display in a rack in the kitchen. They were made in many colors. *(See Kitchen Collectibles chapter.)* Pictured is a place setting of black and white enamelware along with Wm. Rogers Mfg. Co. silverplate silverware, circa 1920s. (Enamelware $5-$8 each; silverware-12 pieces $18-$20).

This wonderful old metal jug would be a conversation piece wherever it was displayed. The lid is heavy glass and the inside liner also appears to be glass. The bottom is marked "ALADDIN INDUSTRIES, INC./ 415/Aladdin/ PATENED IN U.S./NOV. 14, 1922/MADE IN/ CHICAGO, U.S.A." The lid is also marked "Aladdin." ($50+).

The Hawkeye picnic basket (circa 1920s) is also a great cabin collectible. It was made of a ribbed fiber and was lined with galvanized tin. A removable metal ice compartment also was included as part of the basket. The original strap that was used to secure the basket is missing. The Hawkeye baskets were made in Burlington, Iowa, for decades. The oldest baskets are marked with a patent date in the early 1900s. This basket's marking reads "HAWKEYE/ BASKET/REFRIGERATOR/PATENTS PENDING/BURLINGTON IOWA." ($75-$100).

The Hawkeye baskets were still being made in 1939 as shown by this advertisement in the New York-based Bennett Bros. catalog in 1939. The baskets included a "polished metal lining" and a removable ice compartment. Insulation had apparently been added. The baskets were marked "Hawkeye" in large letters on the underside of the cover. The price was listed as $15.00.

During the 1920s and 1930s, gallon jugs were filled with liners made of earthenware. The Sears Fall and Winter 1931-1932 catalog featured a jug called "Cross Country" with this feature. The advertising stated that it would "keep solid food or liquid hot or cold 10 to 12 hours." The jug sold for $1.69. The jug had a steel casing, cork insulation, and a heavy aluminum lid. Folding camp furniture including a chair and stool are also pictured. The chair sold for 98¢ and the stool was priced at 69¢. Both were made from steel and duck, a canvas type material.

This blue gallon jug is similar to the one advertised in the Sears 1931-1932 catalog. Although part of the label is missing, it originally read "THE GENUINE/CAL-O-REX/GALLON JUG/UNITED DRUG CO./BOSTON, MASS." The jug contains the same type lid and handle as those featured on the Sears products. ($30-$40).

The CAL-O-REX jug also includes an earthenware liner as does the Sears example. These liners make the jugs quite heavy.

Very interesting "Little Brown Jug" with label intact. The spout is missing. The pictures feature the jug being used by tourists, a farmer, campers, and for fishing trips. The label reads "PATENTED DEC. 11, 1923/APRIL 1, 1924/OTHER PATENTS PENDING/KEEPS FOODS OR LIQUIDS/HOT OR COLD/MADE ONLY BY/MACOMB MANUFACTURING COMPANY/MACOMB, ILLINOIS." On the bottom is marked "Macomb Manufacturing Company, Macomb, Illinois." Several patent dates are also listed including 1925. This jug also is filled with an earthenware liner. The newer Little Brown jug features a spout at the top (missing its cap) and no earthenware liner. The label reads "Little/Brown Jug/HEMP AND CO./MACOMB, ILL." (Note company name change). (Older, $40+; newer, $15+).

The smaller near mint chest is circa late 1950s-early 1960s and is marked "LITTLE BROWN/CHEST/HEMP AND CO., INC. MACOMB, ILLINOIS U.S.A." The outfit includes a lift-out tray and an ice pick and bottle opener in the lid. ($45-$50).

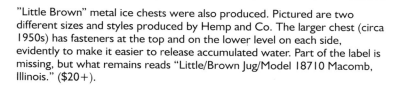

"Little Brown" metal ice chests were also produced. Pictured are two different sizes and styles produced by Hemp and Co. The larger chest (circa 1950s) has fasteners at the top and on the lower level on each side, evidently to make it easier to release accumulated water. Part of the label is missing, but what remains reads "Little/Brown Jug/Model 18710 Macomb, Illinois." ($20+).

Five picnic baskets and two "Stanley" liquid containers decorate a window seat which features an Indian styled camp blanket as a backdrop. Picnic baskets came in a variety of sizes and styles and several can be stacked on a kitchen cabinet or used individually to fill the open space between the tops of cabinets and the ceilings. The baskets make great storage receptacles. The large jug features a spout on the bottom. It is marked "Stanley/Thermal Jug/It Will Not Break"/Landlr/New Britain U.S.A." The smaller quart example is marked "Aladdin Stanley/Mfg by Aladdin Industries, Inc., Nashville, TN." (Baskets, $15-$20 each; large jug, $20-$25; small thermos, $10-$12.)

This interesting old picnic basket includes an insert which hooked to the inside of the basket with galvanized metal. ($20+).

Although this circa 1940s metal jug looks very much like those pictured in the Butler Brothers ad, it does not feature the new fiberglass insulation. The label reads "THE GENUINE/CAL O REX/PLAIN JUG/X657/ REXALL DRUG CO./LOS ANGELES, BOSTON, ST. LOUIS, U.S.A." The bottom of the jug lists a number of patent numbers but no dates. Pictured with the jug is a more recent picnic basket made by Redmon in Peru, Indiana, circa 1960s. It is marked inside the lid. These baskets came in a variety of styles and colors and were sold complete with plastic plates, mugs and stainless steel forks and spoons in a service for six. The handles of the basket are metal. (Jug, $20-$25; basket, $8-$10).

In addition to woven picnic baskets made of a variety of materials, metal baskets were also produced circa 1950s. They came in many colors and designs, although tan and beige are the most common. These "baskets" are not as large as most of the woven baskets and are sturdy enough to provide storage for even heavy items. A stack of these tins can add storage to any room and offer color as well. Cookbooks, hand mixers, or even toasters could be housed in these colorful baskets if shelf or drawer space is at a minimum. Pictured with the metal baskets is a colorful jug with a spout. It is labeled "KILTIE/COLUMBIAN TERRE HAUTE IND. U.S.A." It may also date from the 1950s. (Tan basket, $20; green, $40; jug, $20-$25).

Exterior Accents

Logs can be used for rustic planters as shown in this interesting hand-made example from a home in Colorado.

A simple log bench can provide outside seating in a cabin setting. This one is located along a stream in the Rocky Mountains.

Collectibles can add additional interest to the exterior of a cabin. They can be placed in the yard, on the outside walls, or on porches or decks. While some of these collectibles can be useful, like porch furniture, others are simply decorative. Some of the items should be chosen to complement the natural surroundings. Pieces can be as subtle as old logs cut to make benches or planters, or as eye-catching as an old sleigh or wagon bed. It depends, of course, on the size of the cabin and the acreage involved.

Regardless of size, flowers can play an important role in decorating the yard of any cabin. If planting is difficult because of growing conditions or lack of time, flowers can be placed in pots, then arranged on rocks, tables or benches to make welcoming color accents.

Old bird houses also offer interesting yard decorations. They can be nailed to poles where they can be enjoyed by the cabin owners and visitors as well as the birds.

Many older cabins bear interesting decorations on their outside walls. These include skis, snowshoes, old lanterns, sleds, and signs. Some cabin owners will be reluctant to "spoil" a wall, but these weathered objects do add personality to a cabin.

Porches and decks offer numerous opportunities to decorate with cabin collectibles. Flowers and plants should be considered important additions to these areas, too. Many older objects can be used as "flower pots." Included are coal buckets, banana boxes and other wooden boxes, wheelbarrows, ice cream freezers, buckets, large graniteware, iron pots, old coolers, minnow buckets, and vintage seeders. A little red wagon or a sled can be used as a "holder" for numerous flowerpots on a porch or deck. An old birdcage stand also can act as a "holder" for a large flower arrangement.

An enclosed porch is the ideal place to showcase Old Hickory type furnishings, vintage wicker pieces or primitive twig designs that need protection from the weather to maintain their values. For open porches and decks, the old metal furniture is recommended. Since the current style includes paint flecking and rust, these pieces are especially appropriate for weather-exposed areas. Various metal pieces were produced through the years including gliders, a variety of chair styles, and several sizes of round tables. Old canvas and wood folding furniture that can be stored when not in use is also adaptable to the deck or open porch. For decades, many different styles of this furniture were marketed. The wood Adirondack lounge chairs also could be used on open porches or decks. Since these pieces are usually quite large, perhaps they are best suited for use in the yard or a patio.

When decorating a closed-in porch, skis, snowshoes, antlers, or mounted fish or deer heads can be used for wall decorations. A set of primitive shelves could be filled with a collection of thermos jugs, picnic baskets, or fishing creels to add interest. A porch also makes a good display area for fishing gear, including poles, tackle boxes, nets, old boat motors, and paddles or oars. A collection of watering cans in both child and adult sizes can also add interest to any porch as long as there is some protection from the weather.

A cabin's exterior can be used to help set the tone for a cabin's personality. Together, the selection of porch furnishings, unusual flower arrangements, and the outdoor display of other interesting collectibles, will offer a hint of many other treasures to be found once inside.

Plant filled Ozark Roadside Pottery, circa 1950s, is used to decorate this rock landscaping in Arkansas. The pottery was sold for many years along highways in the Ozarks. Other pottery items included birdbaths and yard ornaments. *From the collection of Bill Brewer.* ($35-$50 each).

One of two antique sleighs which are displayed at the Avalanche Ranch in Redstone, Colorado. An antique lap robe like those often used to keep warm on early sleigh rides is also pictured. (Robe, $65). *Sled courtesy of Avalanche Ranch, Redstone, Colorado.*

This vintage child's picnic table offers an interesting background for potted flowers, as well as large and small watering cans. This kind of arrangement could be used on a deck, open porch, or in the yard of a cabin.

Signs can play an important part in decorating a cabin. Old signs, made of metal or wood, make for interesting exhibits on the inside or outside of cabin walls. Although this sign is currently displayed on the outside of the authors' cabin, it was originally on a cabin purchased by the family some thirty-five years ago. It is always nice to emphasize family memories whenever possible in finding collectibles for a cabin.

Galvanized watering can marked on the bottom "PATENTED/DEC. 3 1912," ($40-$50).

Shutters like this one at the Avalanche Ranch in Redstone, Colorado, which features a pine tree decoration, would add a unique look to the outside decoration of a new or old cabin. These vintage shutters came from a home in New Hampshire. *Courtesy of Avalanche Ranch.*

Old skis make nice decorations to be used on the outside walls of cabins. This family has combined a pair of skis along with a wolf cut out (for their last name) to make an interesting decoration. *Courtesy of Dick and Joyce Wolf.*

Snowshoes can also be used as a focal point on the outsides of cabins. These appear on a cabin at Avalanche Ranch in Redstone, Colorado. *Courtesy of Avalanche Ranch.*

Advertisement for lanterns from the Minneapolis Butler Bros. catalog from September 1936. A lantern similar to the one on the cabin wall is pictured. It was an R.E. Dietz "Monarch" Hot Blast model whose wholesale price was $8.75 a dozen.

A piece of a 1964 license plate reading "Sportsman's Paradise" along with two old lanterns decorate the outside of this older cabin near Rocky Mountain National Park. (Lanterns, $25-$45). *Courtesy of Ruby I. Pettinger.*

An old wagon wheel mounted on a bed of rock leans comfortably against the wall of a rustic cabin. For new cabin owners who don't want to put holes in their outside walls, rustic items can be placed against a cabin to give it more personality. *Courtesy of Chuck and Ann Fuller. ($50+)*

Items as simple as an old wooden barrel and a pitchfork offer an easy way to add interest to an old cabin. (Pitchfork, $25; barrel, $30+). *Courtesy of Jeff Oliver.*

A rustic settee, made of old parts, blends nicely into its new environment as it rests on the porch of an old cabin. *Courtesy of Jeff Oliver. Bench crafted by Doug Harris.*

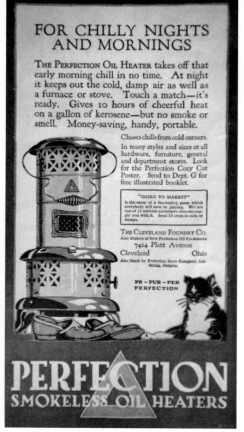

FOR CHILLY NIGHTS AND MORNINGS

THE PERFECTION OIL HEATER takes off that early morning chill in no time. At night it keeps out the cold, damp air as well as a furnace or stove. Touch a match—it's ready. Gives 10 hours of cheerful heat on a gallon of kerosene—but no smoke or smell. Money-saving, handy, portable.

Chases chills from cold corners.

In many styles and sizes at all hardware, furniture, general and department stores. Look for the Perfection Cozy Cat Poster. Send to Dept. G for free illustrated booklet.

"GOING TO MARKET" is the name of a fascinating game which everybody will soon be playing. We are one of 13 national advertisers who can supply you with it. Send 10 cents in coin or stamps.

THE CLEVELAND FOUNDRY CO.
Also Makers of New Perfection Oil Cookstoves
7424 Platt Avenue
Cleveland   Ohio
Also Made by Perfection Stove Company, Ltd.
Sarnia, Ontario.

PR – PUR – PER
PERFECTION

PERFECTION
SMOKELESS OIL HEATERS

This old Perfection oil heater adds interest to a cabin porch along with a potted plant placed on an old twig foot stool. Many of these oil heaters included a brass burner inside that can be made into a lamp. (Heater $65; foot stool $60-$75).

This ad for a Perfection heater appeared in the *Women's Home Companion* in October 1915. The "Smokeless Oil Heaters" were made by the Cleveland Foundry Co. in Cleveland, Ohio. The heater used kerosene for fuel.

A vintage wood banana box holds an assortment of potted flowers to decorate a cabin porch. It rests on the bottom of an old sewing machine stand. Printing on the banana box reads: "PACIFIC FRUIT/& PRODUCE CO./CHEYENNE, WYO./ BANANA BOX." (Banana box, $75; sewing machine stand, $40+).

An old bird cage stand has been converted into use as a flower holder to dress up this cabin porch. The Colorado pillow is old, while the rocker is of recent vintage. (Bird cage stand, $40-$50; pillow, $40).

A full page was devoted to outdoor furniture in the Butler Brothers Spring catalog in 1941. All of these items are now collectible and can be used to give a touch of nostalgia to outdoor areas of a cabin. The folding canvas and wood chairs and the all-metal furniture are especially popular. The metal chairs came in red, green, or blue with white tubing.

Old wheelbarrows or wagons provide unique containers to hold flowers on a cabin deck or porch. This metal wheelbarrow has an iron wheel and frame, along with wood handles. Pictured with it is a vintage folding wood and canvas chair and an old still-working ice cream freezer. The ice cream freezers with wood buckets are very much in demand by rustic decorators. The ice cream freezer is marked "Sterling." (Wheelbarrow, $45; chair, $35+; ice cream freezer $40-$50).

This old red metal chair is similar to the one in the Butler Brothers advertisement. It has stood the test of time well with the help of some repainting. These chairs are presently very popular with both cabin and cottage owners. The current style is to use the chairs in "as is" condition after applying a finish to keep any more paint from flecking. This vintage red Coca-Cola cooler would add a touch of color to any porch arrangement and could be opened to hold flower pots. *Courtesy of Avalanche Ranch, Redstone, Colorado.* (Chair, $30; Coca-Cola cooler, $75).

A very unusual small ice cream freezer is pictured with the more ordinary size. It was made by White Mountain using an outside bucket made of wood and inside pieces of metal. It was probably produced to hold one quart of ice cream. The freezer is so small it would have been difficult to turn the handle. *Small freezer from the collection of Glenn and Douglas Land.*

Wood ice cream freezer tubs need not be discarded after their insides are no longer usable. They can be used to hold a large pot of flowers on a porch cabin or deck. ($10+).

Three children's watering cans are displayed on peg hangers. The watering can with the Indian design was made by the Ohio Art Co. It is marked in a circle "THE OHIO ART CO./MADE IN OHIO/BRYAN OHIO." ($30-$35). The little girl watering can was also an Ohio Art product. It is marked "THE WORLD'S/ (above a globe)/THE OHIO ART CO.(inside the globe)/BEST TOYS/BRYAN OHIO U.S.A." ($30-$35). The butterfly watering can is marked "U.S. METAL TOY/ MFG. CO./MADE IN U.S.A." ($20-$25).

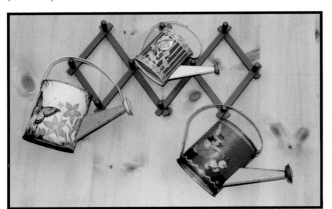

A vintage wood chair is pictured on this cabin porch along with an old seeder now used to hold pots of flowers. (Chair, $35; seeder, $35). *Chair and porch courtesy of Glenn and Douglas Land.*

A wood flower box with horseshoe handles and an old thermos jug with an inside made of earthenware are shown on a cabin porch. The thermos is marked "CAL-O-REX/GALLON JUG/X-634/UNITED DRUG CO./Boston, Mass." and has a handle made of wood and wire. Also pictured is a small folding table. It is marked "......ooklyn Hospital Equip. Co. Inc./Johnstown, PA. Table Bedside." (Thermos, $25+; folding table, $25.) *Flower box and porch courtesy of Wyatt Sabadosh.*

This flower arrangement would be appropriate for either a cabin porch or deck. An unmarked metal bucket holds a pot of flowers while other flowers rest on a galvanized milk container once used for home milk deliveries. It is marked "Dows/Maniti Dairy/Farm." (Bucket, $25; milk container, $30+).

Miscellaneous

In addition to the cabin collectibles already pictured, there remain many other items that can be used to enhance cabin décor. They have been grouped together in this "Miscellaneous" chapter.

One of the most important design considerations is the choice of lamps and light fixtures to complete a cabin's ambiance. Since lighting is both necessary and decorative, the selection of light fixtures and lamps is one of the hardest decisions a cabin owner can make, given the vast selection of new and old products from which to choose. Many of today's cabins use the new light fixtures with steel silhouette designs picturing deer, elk, bears or trees. Other new fixtures made of antlers are also appropriate. *(See Taxidermy and Wildlife Pictorials chapter.)* New lamps using similar patterns and materials are also available. Metal floor and table lamps with amber mica shades can be used effectively in any cabin, as well.

In looking over old photographs of the interior rooms of the Adirondacks "camps" in the early part of the twentieth century, it is interesting to examine the type of lighting that was used. Since there was no electricity, these owners had to rely on kerosene type lights. Shown in these photographs are Rayo and Aladdin lamps, glass hurricane lamps and hanging lamps. Some of the hanging lamps were Victorian in style, featuring flower decorations. In later years, with the addition of electricity, some of the newer "camps" were decorated using Arts and Crafts décor, which featured slag or stained glass light fixtures and lamps. Any of these antique lamps or light fixtures would work well in most cabins. Early Coleman lamps or light fixtures, which have been electrified or vintage wicker floor or table lamps, also can add a rustic look to a cabin. This is especially true if a wicker table or chair is included as part of the décor. Vintage lamps can also be found which were made from the hooves of a deer or elk. Although this type of lamp wouldn't appeal to everyone, these old lamps are readily available.

Rayo type kerosene lamps were used in the early Adirondacks "camps" for much of their lighting needs and are still appropriate for cabin use today. Most of the lamps were nickel plated over brass so many current owners prefer to have the nickel coating removed, the brass polished, and the lamp electrified before it is used as a cabin accessory. The Rayo lamp pictured is marked "Rayo" on the removable cap that covers the opening used to fill the lamp with kerosene. Also shown are two pieces of Roseville pottery. *(See Pinecone Decorated Pottery, Dinner, and Glassware chapter.)* ($75-$100, depending on shade).

Lamps made of peeled logs as well as oak lamps that were once high school shop projects can add to the rustic look. With the current popularity of computers, even weekend cabins may require an office area consisting of a room or corner for computer use. Vintage metal desk lamps made of brass, iron, or other metal make interesting accessories. Some had "goose necks," others were made with slag glass shades while additional models featured metal shades. Harder to find are lamps made with a nautical look. Lamps with a sailboat motif were especially popular in the late 1930s. In addition, vintage western light fixtures can be used in cabins decorated with "the West" in mind. *(See The Western Look chapter.)*

Pictures and mirrors always add interest to a cabin wall, especially now that more and more cabins are using drywall, knotty pine, and other flat surfaces for some of the inside walls. Although pictures relating to wildlife and sports have already been mentioned, many other pictures are available for cabin decorating. Included are scenic landscapes, National Parks scenes, and old hand-colored photographs. Large vintage photographs of real or imagined relatives also give a nostalgic look to any cabin. Unusually framed mirrors also offer a great way to add interest to a wall. Those, which feature twigs, roots, or other natural materials, are especially desirable.

A miniature log cabin used for display can provide both a decorative boost and perhaps the beginning of a collection, as well. Since many different types of log cabins have been made including commercial and hand-made examples, it would be fun to display a variety of models throughout the home. Beginning with a cabin constructed from an old set of Lincoln Logs, a collector could find cabins made as part of play sets, as dollhouses, incense burners, or Christmas houses as well as a never ending supply of hand-made miniature cabins in order to assemble an unusual collection.

Items decorated with pinecone designs would also make a good cabin collection. In addition to the pottery, chinaware, glasses, and kitchen pieces that were produced, bookends, trays, nut dishes, pictures, and other products have been made using the pinecone motif. Just about any kind of a collection, if displayed in an interesting way, can make the cabin decor more intriguing. Cameras, fishing lures, radios, old photographs, dolls equipped with skis or ice skates, ski toys, ice skates, or souvenir pennants are some examples of interesting items that could provide ideas for unique cabin collections.

Lastly, before ending a discussion on cabin collectibles, decorating ideas for the Christmas season are worth mentioning. A cabin or log home offers a unique opportunity to use collectibles that are special to the holiday season and to cabin décor. Sleds, ice skates, pack baskets, camp blankets, and real trees can all be used as part of the decorating scheme. In addition, antique ornaments representing acorns, pinecones, fish, birds, and other animals can be used to decorate a small tree for the Christmas season. An idea for a decorating touch in a cabin located in snow country is to assemble a collection of plastic 1950s Santas on skis or snowshoes in a variety of sizes along with plastic snowmen from the same era. These figures can be combined to make a holiday arrangement for a table top. For a cabin located on or near a fishing lake, vintage fishing lures can add a festive touch when used to decorate a small holiday tree. In any cabin, trees can be decorated using only natural materials like pinecones, twigs, acorns, and dried flowers. Antique and vintage Christmas ornaments and accessories are fun to collect and can always be used to add a festive look to a cabin that will continue to grow in appeal as many of the cabin collectibles pictured in this book are added to its décor.

Another attractive lamp that is also useful is the antique glass oil lamp. Because many cabins are located in areas where electricity can sometimes be out for hours at a time, these lamps offer more and safer lighting than candles. They are readily available at most antique malls and can be found in clear glass models or in fancier colored and patterned glass styles. This blue and white partly frosted lamp was purchased by the authors at a country auction in 1964 for use in a log cabin and is still being used in a family cabin today. The commercially offered lamp oil, instead of kerosene, works well as a fuel. It rests on a round oak table covered with a vintage blue and white tablecloth. (Lamp, $55-$75).

The Montgomery Ward catalog for 1924 included a page of non-electric lamps and light fixtures. Included were Coleman type lamps, wall lamps with brackets, angle lamps, Rayo type lights, and hanging lamps. Hanging lights are also included in the interior photographs of the old Adirondacks camps. Although some of the pictured models are perhaps too fancy for the taste of many cabin owners, the plainer store lamp model would work well in a cabin with rustic furnishings or accents. It was priced at $9.98 in 1924.

The early Coleman gasoline lamps can also be electrified for use in cabin lighting. Most of these lamps included a base that was nickel plated over brass. The nickel plating can be removed as has been done in this pictured lamp or the lamp can be left with its nickel finish. This lamp is marked on the bottom "Coleman Lamp Co./ Wichita, Kansas/Quick Lite." ($75-$100). *From the collection of the Larry Zillner family.*

Light fixtures were also produced using Coleman type lamps. This example has been stripped of its nickel plating, the brass polished, and the fixture electrified. ($250).

Lamps or light fixtures made of oak or brass with slag glass shades also work well with cabin décor. They are especially appropriate when a piece or two of mission oak furniture is used in the room. This large mission art glass lamp is circa 1915 and features an oak base and shade frame with amber marbleized slag glass inserts which emphasize the oak outlined designs. The lamp includes two bulbs placed horizontally. It sits on the top of a vintage oak spool cabinet labeled "Corticelli Silk." *(See also Rustic and Casual Cabin Furniture chapter for other models of similar lamps.)* ($400+).

150B2708— $7.75
Price ......
Shipping weight, 26 lbs.
Paneled Art Glass Lamp. 5½-inch round green glass base. Solid brass frame and arms— 13-inch, green art glass six-panel shade, 4⅝-inch pencil tube fringe with bead trimmings. No. 2 Central Draft embossed, brass oil pot, burner and wick. No. 2 Rochester chimney. Height, 25¼ inches.

The Montgomery Ward catalog from 1916 pictured a paneled art glass lamp. The frame and arms were made of brass, while the glass panels of the shade were green art glass.

150B2742— $9.95
Price ....
Shipping weight, 45 lbs.
Large Art Glass Dome Lamp. 22½-inch six-sided shade and curtain with 6 large panels of green cathedral glass and 6 small panels to match. 4-inch green beaded fringe. Mounted on solid brass frame.
Complete with brass oil fount; No. 2 Central Draft burner and wick; No. 2 Rochester chimney; smoke bell; ceiling canopy and chain. Height, 64 inches.

The 1916 Montgomery Ward catalog advertised a variety of art glass hanging lamps. One of the examples included a six-sided shade with six large panels of green "cathedral" glass and six small matching panels around the bottom. Attached to the edge of the shade was a 4" green beaded fringe. It was mounted on a solid brass frame. This lamp also included a brass oil fount and chimney. It was priced at $9.95 and the cheaper model was only $6.95.

This light fixture circa 1915-1920 also features marbleized amber slag glass in its four brass trimmed shades. The fixture itself is brass. It originally hung in a home in Denver, Colorado. ($600).

Old wicker lamps also work well with cabin décor. This 18" tall lamp has both a wicker base and shade. A metal tag on the bottom of the lamp reads "Pat. Process/Lloyd Loom Products/Baby Carriages & Furniture/ Menominee, Michigan/Method Patented Oct. 16, 1917/Other Patents Pending." An additional paper tag on the bottom adds "The Lloyd Mfg. Co. (Heywood-Wakefield Co.)." It is shown on an oak stand table from the same period. (Lamp, $150).

181

This Heywood Wakefield ad appeared in the *Ladies Home Journal* magazine in June 1926. The Boston firm had already been in business for one hundred years at the time of the ad. The advertisement pictures a desk, chair, and floor model ashtray made of a wicker-type material.

Peeled log-type lamp resting on an "end table" of three stacked suitcases from the 1940s. The handmade lamp is marked "Handcrafted R.A. Volk." Any attractive log lamp is suitable for use as cabin lighting. A new shade has been added to the vintage lamp. The suitcases can be used for storage of photographs, vintage postcards, video tapes, or CDs. The largest suitcase carries a metal tag marked "STYLED FOR/SKYWAY/THE SKY." The middle case is also marked with a metal tag reading "BRIDGEPORT LUGGAGE/ PAKRAFT" along with a small bellhop figure. The smaller, cheaper suitcase is not marked. An interesting oak desk chair with short arms is also pictured. Like the more collectible Stickley and Limbert furniture, this chair is also partially constructed with the use of pegs. (Lamp, $20+; suitcases, $40-$45 each; chair, $100+).

Vintage lamp made of a deer hoof. Old lamps made of elk hooves can also be found. These types of lamps fit nicely in cabins that include vintage animal mounts on the walls. The shade is new. Pictured beside the lamp is a deer figure ashtray made of a composition material. It is marked "Copr. Ornamental Arts & Crafts." This company produced many different deer and elk items in a variety of materials. The old chalk composition-type products are the most desirable. *(See Taxidermy and Wildlife Pictorials chapter.)* A vintage wood humidor with bark trim is displayed on the shelf of the antique oak table. (Lamp, $40-$50; ashtray, $50+; humidor, $30; table, $85.)

With the current use of computers, a cabin may also be in need of vintage desk lamps to enhance the modern look of a computer set up. Vintage goose neck lamps, Arts and Craft style lighting, or other old desk lamp designs can work well. Pictured is an example circa mid to late 1920s. The base is very heavy, perhaps made of iron. The rest of the lamp may be of cast metal. It features an adjustable metal shade. The lamp is finished in an overall design using bronze and brass. ($75+). Also pictured is a small photo album circa 1910 featuring a deer on its cover. ($30) *See also chapter on Furniture.*

Many different kinds of pictures are appropriate to use in decorating cabin walls. These include those featuring wildlife, sports activities, old photographs, and scenery. Shown is a circa 1930 print of the "Holy Cross" mountain located near Minturn, Colorado. This scene can also be found on postcards and steroscopic view cards. (See also Paper Collectibles… chapter and Taxidermy and Wildlife Pictorials chapter.) ($45-$50).

This fireplace mantel décor includes a wonderful old print titled "Flying Stag #147." The original frame was in such disrepair, the print had to be professionally matted and framed. Along with the picture, two Buffalo Pottery plates from their deer series along with vintage oak candlesticks and a large piece of Rocky Mountain pottery have been used to complete the mantel arrangement. A vintage pack basket, filled with camp blankets, a snowshoe, and a handmade pinecone decorated pillow have been added on either side of the gas fireplace. Although wood burning fireplaces are still much more popular for cabin use, many areas restrict their use to reduce air pollution. Gas fireplaces can be used at any time. (Deer print professionally reframed, $200+; plates, $35-$40 each; candlesticks, $45 pair; Rocky Mountain Pottery, $50+; pack basket, $100+; snowshoe, $30; and hand-embroidered pillow, $75).

Old photographs (including hand-tinted) representing mountains, or water as well as other relevant scenery prints can add a sense of tranquility to a cabin's décor. Shown at the top is a vintage photograph with the title written in pencil "Sunset on Fall River" (Colorado). Imprinted on the bottom is "Fine & Coulson/Boulder, Colo." The lower picture is marked "Copyright 1905/Wm. W. Chambers." A river, rowboat, and a man standing on the shore are featured. It is a print of an original hand-tinted photograph similar to the works by Wallace Nutting. (Fall River, $30; Chambers photograph, $50+)

Willow and root fireplace screen, circa early 1900s, from the Jack Rutledge estate. He was a scout for Kit Carson in the early days. This is a wonderful example of the type of work that was popular in the Adirondacks in the early part of the 20th century. If this screen were made for summer use, it would have included a tapestry type insert in the opening. Winter screens were filled with wire mesh. ($1,995). *Courtesy Little Bear's Antique Mall, Glenwood Springs, Colorado.*

Unusual mirrors can also add an interesting touch to cabin walls. This one is a Black Forest-Germany example featuring an intricate design of leaves, twigs, and acorns. ($650). *Courtesy Little Bear's Antique Mall, Glenwood Springs, Colorado.*

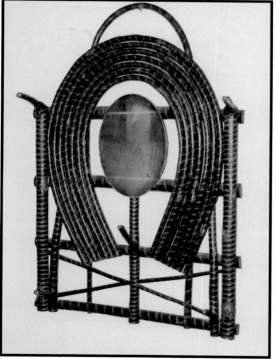

Victorian twig framed mirror which also includes a hat rack. This piece is from the Adirondacks. ($695). *Courtesy Little Bear's Antique Mall, Glenwood Springs, Colorado.*

Old rustic drinking fountain circa 1920 that was originally located on the front porch of the Grand Lake Lodge in Grand Lake, Colorado. It would appear to be the original fixture when the lodge opened in 1920. The rectangle hole at the top used to hold the water spout. A metal section remains above the twig decoration. The piece is currently used as a wall shelf and holds vintage souvenirs. *From the collection of Bob Scott.*

A number of these vintage rustic light fixtures are used for lighting on the front porch at Grand Lake Lodge. After being stored for a number of years, the fixtures were rewired and brought back to life for additional service at the historic lodge. The twig decoration is missing across the bottom. *Courtesy of Grand Lake Lodge, Grand Lake, Colorado.*

A collection of miniature cabins can also add an interesting touch to a cabin. Both commercial and handmade products can be used. Pictured is an unidentified commercial lithographed paper over wood dollhouse cabin circa early 1900s. The cabin has windows covered in blue and red isinglass. The back is opened for play and includes four rooms. 17.25" tall x 18" wide x 9.5" deep. It is displayed on an old oak sewing machine cabinet with a camp blanket on the wall to add color. (Dollhouse cabin, $1,000).

Along with miniature cabins, rustic doll and dollhouse furniture can also be used as accessories. These pieces in a variety of scales were made of bamboo with imitation cane seats. This type of furniture was produced in Japan for decades beginning in the early 1900s. ($5-$15 each piece).

This larger scale set of doll-size hickory furniture is an example of the different styles and sizes of small furniture that was produced through the years. An early Old Hickory Chair Co. catalog featured a four-piece set of Old Hickory doll furniture for $2. It included a settee, rocker, chair, and table. The overall height of the pieces was 9". The style of most of the furniture was that of the "Andrew Jackson" chairs with the rounded back and arms. By 1914, the toy set of hickory furniture was in a simpler design like the chair and settee pictured here. The later four-piece set included two straight chairs, settee, and table, priced at $1.50. (Set of hickory doll furniture, $175).

Pinecone decorated items can always add an outdoor look to cabin décor. These matching unmarked imitation wood pieces are particularly unusual since they have green and white color added to the more traditional brown. Besides bookends and a nut bowl set, a tray or other matching pieces may have been produced. (Bookends, $25; nut bowl set, $20).

Almost any collection can add interest to a cabin room. This assortment of radios from the 1930s and 1940s is displayed on a vintage oak shelf. Many of the radios have been restored to working condition. A Philco radio from the 1940s is housed on the top shelf and a 1940s Emerson example can be seen on the third shelf. Resting on the second shelf is another circa 1940s Philco model that still includes station call letters that were programmed with buttons. Included are WIBW (Topeka, Kansas); WDAF (Kansas City, Missouri); WGN (Chicago, Illinois); KMA (Shenandoah, Iowa); and WHO (Des Moines, Iowa). The radio also had overseas reception available. The circa 1940s radio on the bottom shelf is marked with two letters "M" and "W." This could stand for Montgomery Ward. This radio also still retains several call letters from the period. On the floor beside the shelf on the right is a circa 1930s General Electric model and on the left an unidentified radio also circa 1930s. (The radios range in price from $50-$125 each depending on make, model, and working status).

Both cabin exteriors and interiors offer wonderful opportunities to decorate for the holidays. A red bow adds a festive touch to this old sled. Ice skates, a Christmas wreath, and fresh snow provide finishing touches to this front entrance during the holiday season. (Sled, $45+).

Small pack baskets make wonderful receptacles for Santas, brightly wrapped packages, or other holiday fare. This one is only 12" high. A circa 1960s Santa rests inside. (Pack basket, $75+; Santa, $25).

Cabin related antique Christmas tree ornaments can be collected for decorating a small tree during the holidays. *See Camp Blanket, Quilt and Comforts chapter*. These decorations can include figural ornaments representing fish, birds, other animals, pinecones, and acorns. (Fish, $20+ each; pinecones and acorns, $10+ each).

A worn camp blanket was used to make several Christmas stockings appropriate to use for decorating a cabin fireplace mantel. ($12-$15).

An item that has become quite popular with cabin owners, the nut bowl set, was advertised in the Sears Christmas catalog for 1949. The set sold for $1.00.

Plastic candy holders representing Santas on skis or snowshoes were popular in the late 1940s and 1950s. These Santas, along with the plastic snowmen which were also produced at this time, could be used for decorations on a table top in a cabin located in snow country. Shown are candy holders of this type. (Candy Santas, $20-$25 each; snowmen, $15-$20; boot, $10-$15.)

Several different sizes and designs of the sets were sold but all of them featured natural rustic wood with a bark finish on the outside and a smooth inner surface. Pictured are three different designs of the nut bowls. One set has only two picks while the other has four. The middle bowl is a fancier design and has been filled with pinecones instead of nuts. ($10-$20 each).

This Christmas decoration features a vintage European wood sled marked "DAVOS" on the top. Santas from the 1930s, 1940s and 1950s are also pictured. They include an 18" Santa, circa 1930s, with a molded painted buckram face, mohair wig, and beard, and wearing his original red taffeta suit. The boots are made of heavy plaster-like material. The 19" composition Santa is also circa 1930s. He has painted features along with a molded beard, mustache, and hat. He is jointed at the neck and shoulders but his legs are stationary. He wears molded black boots. The small 13" plush Santa dates from the 1950s. He has a vinyl head with painted features and molded hair, mustache and beard. He still carries his original tag which reads "Knickerbocker/Toy Co. Inc./New York, U.S.A." The largest Santa is 24" tall and is circa late 1940s. He has a plastic mask face, painted features, and a white mohair beard and hair. His suit is red taffeta and he wears shiny black boots and a matching belt of a material similar to oilcloth. (Sled, $75; cloth Santa, $250+; 24" tall Santa, $125+; composition redressed and paint restored Santa, $175+; Knickerbocker Santa, $75-$100).

Sources

Avalanche Ranch in Redstone, Colorado, is located along the scenic Crystal River near Aspen. The property includes log cabin rentals and an award-winning antique shop featuring rustic furniture and collectibles selected by owner Sharon Boucher.

Adirondack Mountains Antique Show at Byron Park
Rt. 28 North, Indian Lake, NY
Includes 130 dealers of camp and lodge materials
Presented by Oliver and Gannon Associates, Inc.
(518) 861-5478

Avalanche Ranch
Sharon Boucher
12863 Hwy. 133
Redstone, CO 81623
(970) 963-2870
www.avalancheranch.com
Specializes in rustic furniture and accessories.

Black Bass Antiques
Lake Shore Dr.
Bolton Landing, NY 12814
(518) 644-2389
www.blackbassantiques.com
Rustic decorative accessories, including fishing memorabilia, canoes, back packs, original prints, and rustic furniture.

Eureka Springs, Arkansas
Home of six antique malls, including many booths which feature rustic and western accessories.

Fighting Bear Antiques
P.O. Box 3790
375 S. Cache Dr.
Jackson Hole, WY 83001
(307) 733-2669
Terry and Sandy Winchell are leading authorities on Thomas Molesworth and an important source for his furniture.

Little Bear's Antique Mall
Nanci & Harvey Gillmore
2802 S. Grand Ave.
Glenwood Springs, CO 81601
(970) 945-4501
Specializes in rustic furniture and accessories.

Little Bear Antiques & Uniques
Nanci & Harvey Gilmore
107 Mill St.
Aspen, CO 81611
(970) 925-3705
Rustic and elegant Mountain Lodge furniture and accessories.

Loveland-Fort Collins, Colorado
Fifteen antique malls and shops, which include dealers selling cabin related accessories. Loveland and Rocky Mountain Pottery were made in Loveland, so examples from these pottery factories can easily be found. Loveland is approximately 25 miles from Rocky Mountain National Park on Highway 34.

Moose America Antiques
Bob Oestreicher
73 Main Street
P.O. Box 1285
Rangeley, ME 049-70
(207) 864-3699
bob.mooseamerica@horizon.net
Specializes in vintage rustic furniture with related cabin accessories. Mail order available upon request.

Old Hickory Furniture Company, Inc.
403 S. Noble Street
Shelbyville, IN 46176
Toll Free: 1 800 232 BARK
Fax: (317) 398-2275
www.oldhickory.com
The Old Hickory Furniture Company still manufactures many of the original furniture designs (including the Andrew Jackson Chair & Rocker) as well as new designs to fit modern times. All of the furniture is currently manufactured in one location in Shelbyville, Indiana in much the same manner as it was 100 years ago.

Palmer Wirfs & Assoc.
2060 N. Marine Dr.
Portland, OR
(503) 282-0877
www.palmerwirfs.com
Shows at Portland Expo Center, March, July, October.

Rose Bowl Flea Market
Second Sunday of every month
Pasadena, CA
R.G. Canning-Shows & Events
(323) 560-7469 event ext. 11
www.rgcshows.com
World's Largest Flea Market.

Bibliography

Altman, Violet and Seymour. *The Book of Buffalo Pottery.* West Chester, Pennsylvania: Schiffer Publishing, Ltd., 1969 and 1987.

Brownstein, Jerry and Kathy. *Beacon Blankets Make Warm Friends.* Atglen, PA: Schiffer Publishing, Ltd., 2001.

Cameron, Elisabeth. *Encyclopedia of Pottery & Porcelain 1800-1960.* New York, N.Y.: Facts on File Publications, 1986.

Clark, Michael E., Jill Thomas-Clark. *The Stickley Brothers.* Layton, Utah: Gibbs Smith Publisher, 2002.

Couch, Joanne. "Old Hickory Has Barrel of Fun Making Furniture." *Sunday Tribune and Star Courier.* Bloomington, Indiana, August 17, 1969.

Cox, Susan N. *Antique Trader Books 20ᵗʰ Century American Ceramics Price Guide.* Dubuque, IA.: Antique Trader Publications, 1996.

Eden Sterling Company. Flemish Art Co. Catalogue (Reprint). Cincinnati, Ohio: Eden Sterling Company, 2002.

Ewald, Chase Reynolds. *Cowboy Chic: Western Style Comes Home.* Salt Lake City, Utah: Gibbs Smith Publisher, 2000.

Falk, Sally. "Rustic Furniture." *The Indianapolis Star,* June 24, 1984.

Flood, Elizabeth Clair. *Cowboy High Style: Thomas Molesworth to the New West.* Salt Lake City, Utah: Gibbs Smith Publisher, 1992.

Florence, Gene. *Collectors Encyclopedia of Depression Glass.* Lexington, KY.: Collectors Books, 2000.

Gilborn, Craig. *Adirondack Furniture and the Rustic Tradition.* New York, N.Y.: Harry N. Abrams, Incorporated, 1987.

Humphery, Corinne. "High-Style Skis." *Log Home Living.* Dec. 1999.

Husfloen, Kyle. *Antique Trader Pottery & Porcelain Ceramics Price Guide, 3ʳᵈ Edition.* Iola, WI.: Krause Publications, 2000.

Huxford, Sharon. *The Collectors Encyclopedia of McCoy Pottery.* Dallas, TX.: Taylor Publishing Company, 1980 and 1982.

Huxford, Sharon and Bob. *The Collectors Encyclopedia of Roseville Pottery.* Paducah, KY.: Collector Books/Schroeder Publishing Co., Inc., 1980 and 1997.

Klatt, Mary Beth. *U.S.A. Weekend.* "Collectors are Hot for the Imperial Chambers." Jan. 17-19, 2003.

Kovel, Ralph and Terry. *Kovels on Antiques and Collectibles.* "Winter Sports." Palm Coast, Fla., February 2002.

Kylloe, Ralph. *A History of the Old Hickory Chair Company and the Indiana Hickory Furniture Movement Revised and Updated in 2002.* Lake George, N.Y.: Published by Ralph Kylloe Antiques and Rustic Publications, 1995 and 2002.

Kylloe, Ralph. *Rustic Traditions.* Salt Lake City, Utah: Gibbs Smith Publisher, first paperback edition 1995.

Lehner, Lois. *Lehner's Encyclopedia of U.S. Marks on Pottery, Porcelain and Clay.* Paducah, KY: Collector Books, 1988.

Linoff, Victor M. *Rustic Hickory Furniture Co. Porch, Lawn and Cottage Furniture Two Complete Catalogs, ca. 1904 and 1926.* New York, N.Y.: Dover Publications, Inc., 1991.

Mack, Daniel. *Log Cabin Living.* Salt Lake City, Utah: Gibbs Smith Publisher, 1999.

Martinsville Daily Reporter. Martinsville, Indiana: "Fire Destroys Part of Factory," July 9, 1968; "Miles Bros. Hope for Higher Quality Growth," January 23, 1970; "'Old Hickory A-go-go' Declares New Management," December 23, 1965; "Old Hickory Buy Barrel Equipment," November 9, 1970; "Old Hickory's Closing Makes More Unemployed," July 8, 1978; "Old Hickory Merges with Ramada Inns," December 10, 1968. Picture captions including Old Hickory information: December 1968; January 7, 1972; December 1976.

Molesworthtoo.com/granddad.html. Web site information on Thomas Molesworth from grandson Leslie Molesworth-Callahan.

Murphy, Dudley and Rick Edmisten. *Fishing Lure Collectibles: An Identification and Value Guide to the Most Collectible Antique Fishing Lures.* Paducah, KY: Collector Books, 1995.

"Old Hickory Company Has Changed Name." *Martinsville Republican.* Martinsville, Indiana. February 8, 1921.

O'Leary, Ann Stillman. *Adirondack Style.* New York, N.Y.: Clarkson Potter, 1998.

Schroy, Ellen T. *Warman's Antiques and Collectibles Price Guide 37ᵗʰ Edition.* Iola, WI.: Krause Publications, 2003.

Smith, Bruce and Yoshiko Yamamoto. *The Beautiful Necessity: Decorating with Arts & Crafts.* Salt Lake City, Utah: Gibbs Smith Publisher, 1996.

Stuttgen, Joanne Raetz. *Martinsville A Pictorial History.* G. Bradley Publishing, Inc., 1995.

Ward, Betty and Nancy Schiffer. *Weller, Roseville and Related Zanesville Art Pottery and Tiles.* Atglen, PA.: Schiffer Publishing Ltd., 2000.

Zeisel, Eva Web site. Schein-Joseph International Museum of Ceramic Art. "Lost Molds and Found Dinnerware: Rediscovering Eva Zeisel's Hallcraft."

Index